EXPANDING the Living Space in Your Home

Perma-Shield casement windows by Andersen Corporation, Bayport, Minnesota

RESTON PUBLISHING COMPANY, INC.
A Prentice-Hall Company
Reston, Virginia

EXPANDING *the Living Space in Your Home:*

A GUIDE TO REMODELING BASEMENTS, ATTICS, GARAGES & PORCHES

L. Donald Meyers & Richard Demske

Library of Congress Cataloging in Publication Data

Meyers, L. Donald
   Expanding the living space in your home.

   Includes index.
   1. Dwellings—Remodeling.   I.   Demske, Richard,
joint author.   II.   Title.
TH4816.M49   643'.5   76-11744
ISBN 0-87909-228-9

© 1976 by Reston Publishing Company, Inc.
   A Prentice-Hall Company
Reston, Virginia   22090

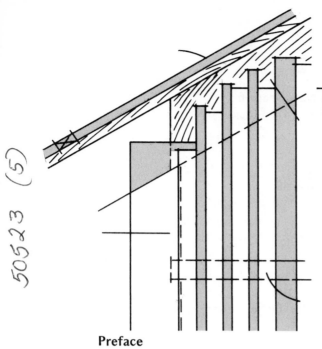

Table of Contents

Preface

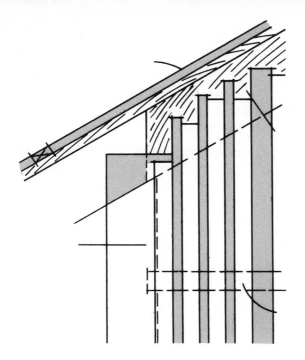

Preface

"We need more room." A common complaint among homeowners, which often means uprooting the family for a larger—and much more expensive—place in the suburbs. Before you take this serious course of action, it is wise to carefully consider the alternatives. Perhaps you can add onto your present home somehow—and perhaps not. Such additions depend on zoning and building regulations, on your finances, and on the type of house you own. (See Chapter 1 for the trade-offs to consider before you make any committments.)

For many families, the most convenient and least expensive course is to add *in*, rather than on. Take stock of the living area you have now. Can a little-used dining room, for example, be converted to either a den or a library? Is there even greater potential in a barren attic, a cluttered basement, an underutilized garage or porch? These areas are already closed in from the elements, require minimal rough construction, and ordinarily need no construction permits or building code inspections. And usually they do not add additional property taxes, a most important consideration in these days of ever-increasing municipal levies.

This book helps you to assess the possibilities of all these alternatives, tells you how to finance and construct them, and then *x*   gives you some pointers on how to decorate your new-found space. For many people, expanding the living space in your present home is a worthwhile and easy-to-do endeavor.

*   *   *

The authors wish to thank the many trade associations and building supply manufacturers who helped make this book possible.

L.D.M.
R.D.

EXPANDING *the Living Space in Your Home*

The Economic Facts of Living Space

In 1972, there was a flourishing housing industry. But then along came "stagflation," an economic period wherein prices rose and income declined—to the considerable consternation of those economists who embraced the "inflexible" law of supply and demand. Home building fell from 2.4 million units in 1972 to considerably less than one million during 1975.

Contrary to the precepts of the practitioners of the "dismal science," the supply of homes diminished sharply, even as the demand for them became more and more acute. As prices rose, the demand for money rose, resulting in "disintermediation," a drain of dollars from the financial institutions that finance mortgages into more profitable forms of investment. As the money flowed out, savings banks and savings and loan associations found their mortgage funds shrinking to virtually nothing. With mortgages available only at extremely high interest rates, there were very few buyers for homes.

Now, it would seem logical that with very few families able to buy homes, those persons selling homes would mark down their prices as an inducement for those prospective buyers who were in the wings of the housing market, waiting for interest rates to fall.

Wrong. The easier way was to simply cut back on building, raise the prices of those homes that were built, and lay off the workers who were in the home-building trades. Now *that* was a way to bring down prices—by contributing to a recession. (Following the same inexorable logic, the auto manufacturers—having raised prices

4   an average of $500 on 1975 models and watched demand, unsurprisingly, fall off—laid off factory workers and raised the prices of cars even higher.)

At any rate, with few houses being built, and more and more people entering the housing market each month, it is not at all amazing that the demand for the few houses available pushed up prices even more, with the equally unstaggering consequence that the middle-class Americans who make up the vast bulk of the housing market were priced right out of contention.

ADDING ON TO HOUSE SPACE

The simple fact is that the good old days are over. There was a time that you simply packed and moved when you outgrew your house. Not any more. Very few of us can afford it.

So when a cottage built for two bursts its seams with a family of six, what do you do? There is really only one answer for those who cannot afford to move—and that is expansion.

The word *expansion* immediately calls to mind *addition*, but this is only one method of expansion. Although it will raise the value of your home and give you some eminently usable living space, a home addition is quite expensive. It costs as much as, and often more than, the same amount of square feet in a new home. And although it will add to the value of your home, the added value may be considerably less than the cost of the addition. This is particularly true if your home is already worth the top price for your neighborhood.

Suppose, for example, that you live in an area where homes sell for $25,000 to $35,000. If your home is worth close to $35,000 now, how much more will it sell for if you tack on a $10,000 addition? A ball park figure is $40,000—probably less. (On the other hand, a $10,000 addition to a $25,000 home in the same neighborhood may return close to the entire $10,000.)

There are other drawbacks to home additions. There may not be room on your lot, for example. Or it may look like there is room, but municipal setback regulations prevent you from going any closer to the property line.

One of the most serious objections to adding a room is that it may *look* added on. Even the humblest of homes has a certain architectural integrity that is often jarred by an extra room tacked onto the side or the rear. If you do plan a room addition, it is wise to have an architect at least check the drawings.

INTERIOR EXPANSION

There are other ways to expand other than out—or up. You can expand *in*. Look at your home. Is all the space used efficiently?

Figure 1-1: Cluttered, underutilized basement becomes useful living area after remodeling (*courtesy of Masonite Corporation*).

6   Do you really need all the attic space for storage? Is the basement serving any purpose other than as a place to keep summer furniture? And how about the attached garage? And what about that old porch or carport?

It may be that you use the garage all the time. But how much harm, really, can the elements do to a car with a modern automotive finish? Maybe you'd be better off leaving it outside and converting the garage to a family room where the kids can play and entertain (and leave you in peace in the living room). Sure, the breezeway is nice on a hot summer day, but wouldn't it be nicer all year round? What would you do with all that junk in the basement if you made a recreation room there? *Junk* it, of course.

Don't the same cautions apply to internal expansion as to additions? Yes, they do. Yes, you can overimprove and overprice your home. Yes, interior improvements are expensive. In some

Figure 1-2: Typical attic area is seen before remodeling.

Figure 1-3: After remodeling, same area is a combination bedroom-playroom for two children.

cases—basements, in particular—you may get little or nothing back in resale value.

But there are significant differences that make interior space-gaining improvements a much better deal than additions or similar improvements. First of all, usually you do not need a building permit. Also, even though the cost of materials is the same, you avoid such very expensive and difficult tasks as breaking into the existing structure, pouring new foundations or footings, and applying new roofing. Even more important, the necessary work, discussed in the following chapters, is relatively easy to do yourself.

It is not that additions are any more difficult *per se*, but they require more involved planning, skill, and know-how. Furthermore, interior improvements can ordinarily be done at your own pace. If you're breaking into a wall of your home, you had better finish before bad weather starts. And there is an urgency to getting the roof on the new structure because of the elements. (Once an addition is enclosed and roofed in, then it *becomes* an interior improvement.)

WHAT WILL IT COST?

It is always hazardous to discuss price in view of the discrepancies at different times between different parts of the country, but the average 1975 costs listed below will give you some basis for comparison. (The costs assume that you do most of the work.)

Basement

The usual improvements include putting up several partitions, adding extra heating and lighting, applying floor tile, installing paneling, and putting up some sort of ceiling. A bar, usually without running water, is ordinarily part of the basement recreation room plan. The typical materials cost averages $5–$6 per square foot, and more if you get into a wet bar, toilet facilities, or other extras. Figure on spending at least $1,500–$2,500.

Attic

If you're just making an extra bedroom or two, utilizing existing windows, all you'll need are walls, a floor, and a ceiling, plus

Figure 1-4: Other end of attic room shown in Figure 1-3 features prefabricated fireplace in left foreground and is comfortable for reading and leisure activities (*courtesy of Armstrong Cork Company*).

some extensions to your electrical and heating systems. This shouldn't run any more than $4–$5 per square foot. However, if you must add dormers to provide sufficient headroom or illumination, add another $800 or so for each running foot of frontage. If you don't already have a decent stairway, figure on an additional $600–$700 to improve it. A half bath will run close to $2,000.

Garage

You will probably have to add some windows. Then there's the problem of doing something with the old driveway and garage doors. You will have to wall off the area and provide a standard door opening instead, or perhaps put in some sliding doors or a large window. Walls, and preferably floors, must be insulated, but not much framing is required. You will probably want to build up the floor with "dead men" (lumber shims) to allow for insulation. Plan on about $8–$10 per square foot.

Figure 1-5: Garage remodeling gives house a better exterior and adds usable room. Note too that the garage-turned-family room gives a larger, more horizontal look to the structure. It was expensive, however, to remove the old driveway and replace it with sod (*courtesy of Masonite Corporation*).

Porch, Carport, or Breezeway

Any of these projects demands enclosing one or more sides. Exterior walls, with insulation and siding, add to the cost, as do windows and doors. Most such rooms will be small, which makes for a smaller overall cost but high per-foot charges. The guess is even rougher here, but plan on proportionately more than the other projects—roughly $10–$12 per square foot, or $1,000 and up depending on the size.

Extras—Their Costs

The figures given above are rough approximations for noncontracted work and don't take into consideration the cost of your own labor or of such expensive extras as bathroom or kitchen facilities. If you have these in mind (and if you *need* them, they are a good investment), the figures are much higher than the ones mentioned. A small full bath put in by a contractor could easily cost $5,000 all by itself. If you're considering an apartment with even a minimal kitchen, figure on at least another $5,000 for the kitchen alone. (You don't save too much on these expensive-materials jobs by doing them yourself.)

Figure 1-6: Old-fashioned loveliness is reflected in this basement's new brick fireplace surrounded by ponderosa pine.

Figure 1-7: A less expensive but handsome "extra" is this metal free-standing fireplace with Royal Woodgrain paneling (*courtesy of Evans Products*).

Fancy wet bars, fireplaces, and similar embellishments raise the price up frightfully (at least $500, and maybe $1,500). And add 50–150% if you hire somebody to do these jobs for you.

Figure 1-8: Extras such as a bar add interest and party conveniences to a basement remodeling—but they are rather costly (*courtesy of Marlite Paneling*).

12   DO IT YOURSELF?

Because it is important, it should be emphasized that virtually all of the space-gaining renovations discussed here are within the capabilities of a reasonably experienced do-it-yourselfer. A great many of the jobs (installing flooring, paneling, and ceiling tile, for example) can be accomplished by a rank amateur.

How much can you save by doing it yourself? That depends on how labor-intensive the job is. A job that involves mostly materials, like installing bathroom fixtures, isn't much cheaper if you do the work. But something like wall framing that consists of relatively cheap wood (and relatively expensive labor) can result in a considerable saving as a do-it-yourself project.

Fortunately, the materials required for most of the finishing-off jobs discussed here are comparatively inexpensive, and you can save half or more on costs by doing most of the jobs yourself. When you get into expensive materials such as exterior doors, windows, plumbing fixtures, electrical appliances, etc., you save considerably less. As a very rough guide, figure on saving 50–60% of the contractor's cost—more for the labor-intensive jobs, less for high-materials jobs. The question of whether it's worth *your* while,

Figure 1-9: Labor-intensive jobs are rendered easy and inexpensive by new installation methods such as this employing direct-attachment spring clips for ceiling tiles (*courtesy of Armstrong Cork Company*).

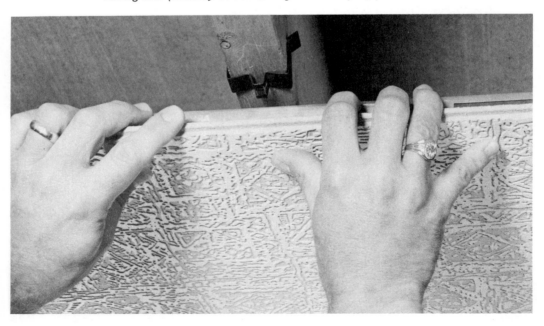

though, depends on your income versus what it would cost to have skilled laborers perform the job. One way to look at it is that for those in the 30-35% income tax bracket, your savings after taxes is from $5–$10 an hour. (To pay a $12-an-hour carpenter, for example, you must earn about $17 an hour before taxes.)

On the other hand, if you *are* earning that much, is it worth it to spend so much time working around the house—or would you be better off sticking to your regular job where you can earn the big dollars? Once again, we have a problem for the dismal scientists of economics—and they don't have any better answers than we do. Only you can decide that.

EFFECT ON RESALE PRICE

It should be conceded at the outset that the type of improvements discussed in these pages will not necessarily add to the resale value of your home. If resale were the only criterion, then an addition would be a much better deal (about a two-thirds return, on the average).

The value added by finishing off a basement, for example—no matter how elaborate—is virtually zero. In most areas, similar homes—one with a finished basement, one without—sell for approximately the same price. A better-than-average job may result in a financial return, if you're lucky, of perhaps 1/3 of what you put into it (excluding labor).

At the other end of the scale, a finished attic (ordinarily turned into extra bedrooms) can return almost all of the materials investment upon sale. Converted garages and porches may add 50–75% of their cost to the value of your house, and perhaps a little more if the house itself is small and the extra space means a lot more room.

THE REAL VALUE

If the economic realities of resale have depressed you, take heart. The bad news should be disposed of first. Did you really expect to get every penny back? Is resale the reason you are considering this type of job to begin with? If you can increase the value of your home, so much the better, but the primary reason you are looking into expansion is simply that you need more room, and you need it badly enough to think about investing a lot of extra work and money. If you wanted to move, you would have. (And then you'd be reading another of our books, *Your Home: Buying,*

14   *Building, and Financing*, Reston, Va.: Reston Publishing Company, Inc., 1975.)

Obviously, you like it pretty well where you are or you can't afford to move, or you have some other cogent reason for staying. And there are a lot of excellent reasons—like not wanting to pay real estate commissions, closing fees, and other transfer costs. Another good reason for staying where you are is that you have an excellent, low-interest mortgage and don't want to trade it in for a much more expensive one. And maybe you've looked at the price of houses lately. (If you haven't, do so.) Even though you might lose money on the improvement itself, the overall economic tradeoffs—the cost of staying and expanding versus the cost of moving—are usually quite favorable.

To make the choice to stay, however, you should also consider the entire real estate picture. If your neighborhood is going to the dogs, it doesn't make much sense to invest any more money than is necessary to keep your own house in reasonable repair. If the state is putting an expressway through your property in a few years, further investment is foolish.

Assuming you have a nice house in a nice neighborhood, it makes very good economic sense to convert dead space to living area and stay put. And economics is just one consideration. Even though kids eventually adjust to new surroundings, there is always temporary heartbreak. Adults may *think* that they will be just as happy in a new neighborhood, but it doesn't always happen that way. Do you really think that you'll keep seeing old neighborhood friends? The odds are heavily against any form of communication except a brief guilty note in a Christmas card.

If it's been a long time since you last moved, you are no doubt ill-prepared for the assorted little traumas that go with it. Preparing the house for sale is one example. You'll have to clean out the closets, the attic, the basement, and the garage to make them look as large and uncluttered as possible. And every time someone calls to look at the house, the mad scramble to pick up the papers, clean the dishes, and make the place otherwise tip-top will strain your nerves beyond imagining.

We haven't even mentioned the move itself. The cost is one thing; the packing is another—and wait until you discover how much junk you've collected all these years! Start with the children's toys, for example, and see which ones they're willing to part with. This alone may make you decide to stay.

Planning & Paying for Your Project

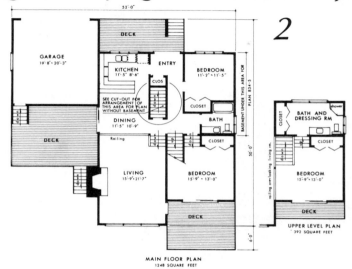

2

MAIN FLOOR PLAN
1248 SQUARE FEET

UPPER LEVEL PLAN
392 SQUARE FEET

You wouldn't be considering any of the projects in this book unless you had some idea of the sort of improvement you want. A new family member often compels an urgent search for another bedroom. The kids' music has Mom and Dad up the wall, so that a recreation room becomes a psychological necessity. There is really no place for the family to gather informally, and a family room becomes eminently desirable.

For one reason or another, you have already rejected moving to a new house, and have concluded that it would be wise to finish off the basement or attic, close in the porch, or whatever. What's the next step? Money, of course. Preliminary checking has probably indicated that the cost will be more than you thought it would be—but don't get discouraged. There are ways. First of all, this book will show you all you need to know to do the entire job yourself. That'll save plenty. And if you don't want to do it all (or don't think you can), farm out just the parts of the job that worry you. Not everyone is comfortable with electrical work, so hire out just that one job—or only the part that scares you. Maybe, for example, you feel confident of your wiring prowess but don't want to make the hookup to the hot fuse box. There are plenty of licensed electricians who will be glad to check your work and make the connection—and maybe even give you some pointers.

Don't forget, too, that when you're doing it yourself, you can work not only at your leisure but also with your paycheck. When

Figure 2-1: If the purpose of your remodeling project is recreation and additional living space, a family room like this would be a great idea (*courtesy of Mazonite Corporation*).

you can afford it, buy a load of framing lumber, then the paneling next time around, then the tile later on, etc. If worse comes to worse (and it often does), your neighborhood bank may be willing to give you a home improvement loan.

DEFINING THE PURPOSE OF THE NEW SPACE

Some remodeling projects are quite easy to plan. A small attic, for example, may have room for one bedroom and that's all.

Figure 2-2: A fireplace and lots of seating are almost mandatory in any new space you make for just sitting and relaxing (*courtesy of American Plywood Association*).

You still have to do a lot of planning, but you've already passed beyond the first step of overall design.

If you have a large attic or are planning to convert your basement into a living area, it may not be quite as simple as you originally thought. Suppose that you only need one extra bedroom, but have a large attic. Should you just go ahead and build one large bedroom, or maybe make it into two or more? How about a bathroom? Do you have room? Can you connect a new bathroom to existing plumbing at reasonable cost? Your immediate need may be for just one bedroom, but might there be more little people later? And although your youngster may not mind coming downstairs to use the bathroom, the lack of an upstairs bathroom may be quite a negative factor on resale.

Consider the basement. Your purpose here may be simply to

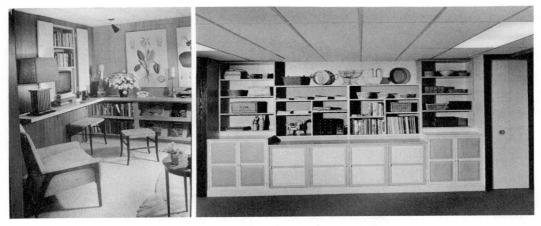

Figure 2-3: New reading space can mean abundant shelving and counter space for books and magazines as well as handy storage built-ins (*courtesy of American Plywood Association*).

get the teen-agers out of your hair, but how about the old folks? Will you want to entertain down there occasionally? If so, what about a bar? And as long as you're going to all that trouble, should you partition off a section for a sewing room? And what about a workshop area? You'll surely need at least a workbench and a place for tools somewhere.

A family planning session will help provide ideas and prevent disasters. You may find, for example, that your ideas and those of your children clash so violently that creating a single recreation room will only add to the bickering, instead of alleviating it. How about two smaller rooms (with a sliding door in between)? You may also realize that the basement room you had in mind will result in the loss of valuable laundry space. Or you may discover that the teen-ager whose bedroom you planned has a real fear of sleeping in the attic.

If you consult with everyone early enough, all of these problems can be avoided, however. And a little discussion and compromise will resolve most conflicts.

IDEAS FOR BASEMENTS

A remodeled basement almost always includes a recreation room. The reason for this is simple: It is out of the way, keeping the noise and the mess out of sight, if not out of mind. Teen-agers and their friends can congregate here away from the "prying" eyes of their parents.

Even though your primary thought in finishing the basement
is to provide a recreation area, remember that there's a lot of open
space down there. A full basement under a one-story home can
double the living area when finished off. Basements in some ranch
homes are long enough to accommodate a couple of bowling lanes.

Before you go downstairs and start putting up studs, make a
rough drawing of the area, including the heating unit and all other
places that you'll have to work around. Compute the approximate
number of square feet. You'll probably be surprised at how much
available space there is.

There is no sense in building a larger recreation room than
you need. Besides being costly, oversized rooms tend to be cold and
barn-like. Smaller rooms are warmer and more intimate. If you
would like a large area to entertain in, it is better to break it up into
several rooms or well-defined areas with dividers or other visual
separators. (Visit a few well-decorated taverns for ideas on this.)

But don't forget the other uses for basement space while
you're doing all this grand decorating. A laundry room, or a
combination laundry-sewing room with lots of built-ins, is a natural
for basements. And allow plenty of room for a workshop. How
about a separate playroom for the small children, or a music room

Figure 2-4: The most common use of attic space is for an extra bedroom, usually for children but it can also become an attractive adult bedroom (*left, courtesy of Armstrong Cork; right, courtesy of Wallcovering Industry Bureau*).

Figure 2-5: A big basement workshop offers excellent space for tools (*courtesy of Masonite Corporation*).

Figure 2-6: Find out how much basement space you have to work with, then divide it into interest areas—perhaps like those in the plan. Note the outside access for bringing lumber and materials into the workshop (*courtesy of Bilco Company*).

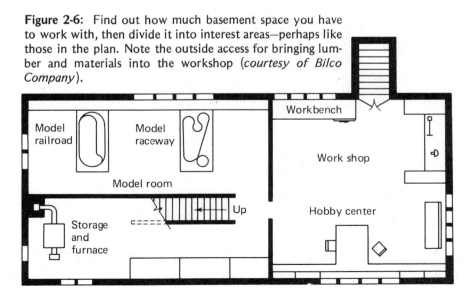

for teen-agers? There is no reason why you can't build a bedroom in the basement, although one bedroom there does tend to seem isolated. Why not two of them?

Other possibilities include a library or any of the other types of rooms mentioned under attic ideas. One exception might be the separate apartment. Unless there is a severe housing shortage in your area, you may have trouble renting a place where people will spend most of their time underground. But it might be a nice private place for an older relative—and it's safer than the attic. Installing a kitchen should be no great problem in a basement apartment. It is relatively easy to install a private entrance, too.

Figure 2-7: Excellent use of basement space is demonstrated here: a refrigerator and stove are hidden behind the bar (*left, above*), a hinged train board is attached to a wall (*right, above*) and the same unit in use has the train board folded out of the way (*immediately below*) and (*below left*) a movable divider on casters permits varying area arrangements in a room.

Figure 2-8: "Expanding" the space in your basement can easily provide an efficient sewing corner.

Figure 2-9: The purpose of this room needs no explanation. Suggestion for parents: add a door at the foot of the stairs and ceiling insulation to contain sound within this "teen-agers haven."

Whether you put in just a recreation room or a complete apartment, a half bath (a full bath for apartments) should be part of your plan. Most plumbing suppliers carry a line of toilets and even bathtubs that empty into the wall, requiring no below-grade plumbing.

Depending on what other storage area is available, you may want to leave a part of your basement unfinished so that you can still have a place to pile the inevitable "junk" that everyone seems to collect as he goes along. This area should be walled off, of course, far out of the sight of guests.

IDEAS FOR ATTICS

As discussed, the attic area is usually made into bedrooms, but seriously consider adding at least a half bath if you can locate it close to the plumbing below. Even if you have to run the lines over a

Figure 2-10: A pleasant sewing "center" can be incorporated easily and inexpensively in the new-found space of a large attic bedroom (*courtesy of Masonite Corporation*).

24 bit, the extra bath will greatly improve the usefulness of this floor and help enormously on resale.

Expandable story-and-a-half houses and Cape Cods are both made specifically for expansion of the upper story. Hopefully, the builder has run the pipes to the expansion area so that putting in a bath is quite simple and less expensive. When money is a problem, settle for a half bath (without a tub or shower).

Instead, you may wish to convert the attic, if it is a large one as in many older homes, to an apartment. The apartment may be used for income, but most of the time it is too difficult and/or prohibitively expensive to provide separate access from the outside. Otherwise, the tenants will have to enter through your quarters. Zoning laws can be quite strict about income apartments, and the building code may require an ugly fire escape even if such renovations are allowed. Many families ignore the law, and make an income apartment in the attic without notifying the authorities. This is quite risky, as neighbors have been known to do the notifying on

Figure 2-11: This view of the room shown on the previous page illustrates how a successful space conversion can provide an all-purpose room as well as attractive guest accomodations (*courtesy of Masonite Corporation*).

their own. Whatever you do, provide some means of escape in case of fire. This is a good idea for any upstairs living area, but particularly third floors, where it is almost as dangerous to jump out as to stay.

The most common and successful way to utilize such an apartment is for elderly relatives. Such an apartment need not necessarily have a separate access, since the tenants are part of the family. This way relatives still have a private place to call their own, and if they take their meals with the rest of you, kitchen facilities aren't necessary.

Because of the added fire hazard for upstairs facilities, it is wise not to introduce any more dangers than are absolutely necessary. Never use anything but grounded UL-approved wiring, and don't allow open space heaters, hot plates, or other dangerous appliances upstairs. Unless a kitchen is vital, try to avoid it. It'll save lots of money as well as worry.

Perhaps the biggest difficulty in attic remodeling is supplying the necessary heat or air conditioning, depending on the region. Ample insulation is essential, of course, but you will need more than that, depending on the size of the new room(s). A small room or two can often be added onto an existing hot water or steam zone, or tapped into an existing duct, although adjustments will have to be made to the rest of the system. Large areas, however, will usually need an extra circulator to provide an additional zone, or even a new, larger heating unit. It is also possible to add another wall-type electric heater. Chapter 9 discusses these problems and their solutions in greater detail, and you can usually get good free assistance from your local utility or fuel supplier. The one thing you must *not* do is add an open space heater.

You can, of course, use the attic for a recreation room or a study, but these are usually better located downstairs. Attics are fine, though, for an artist's studio. Here, a skylight would be a valuable extra. Also, consider such uses as a library, toy room, or student loft.

IDEAS FOR GARAGES

A garage is best suited for conversion to a family room. Because it is usually situated on the same floor as the kitchen and the other living areas, it is an excellent place to put the TV, stereo, piano, or whatever may be the focus of family life. The line between a *family room* and a *recreation room* is rather fine, but you might draw the distinction as between quiet and noisy activities. The recreation room is mainly for games like ping-pong, pool, darts, or

26   whatever. A garage is fine for these activities, too, but the room should be well insulated from the quieter parts of the home. The family room is usually for conversation, listening, TV viewing, and other nonphysical activities. This is a somewhat blurry dividing line,

Figure 2-12: This little-used garage was turned into a family's pleasant sitting-room.

to be sure, and many families combine the two types of activities into a single "family-recreation" room.

Other potential garage uses are a study, a library, a studio or even an office for the owner of a small business or the professional. (Watch for zoning, though.) If it is large enough, the garage is also a perfect place for an apartment.

If your home has no basement, a garage may be the only place for a workshop. If you're like many others in the same predicament, you start off by using a small corner, and gradually expand until the car gets pushed out by a radial arm saw or the like. If you've gone that far, why not just close the place up and use it permanently as a workroom?

One big question in a garage remodeling is what to do with the car. Your car is probably a lot hardier than you give it credit for. But if the weather is bad and space permits, you can at least keep rain and snow off the car by building a carport in front of, or next to, the old garage. (Ironically, someday you might wind up closing that in, too.)

A bath is probably unnecessary in a simple garage renovation. An exception would be when you convert it to an apartment, and even then a member of the family can use your downstairs bathroom, if you have one. Installing a bath in the garage can be expensive because the plumbing is usually rather far away, and it can be difficult getting the right pitch on the drains. If you want an apartment to provide extra income, you'll have to install a full bath, which is really not a great problem as long as you're willing to pay. Separate access, at least, will be much easier than for an attic or basement apartment.

IDEAS FOR PORCHES, CARPORTS, AND BREEZEWAYS

Porches, carports, and breezeways are normally quite small, and most of them will be limited to one room. Porches, depending on their size, can be bedrooms or sitting rooms (family rooms, recreation rooms, or whatever). Carports usually fall into the same category as garages, except that they are ordinarily much smaller and are thus unsuitable for apartments. Breezeways are the smallest of all, and are useful only for small dens, TV rooms, photographic dark rooms, or hobby rooms of some kind. In some homes, breezeway remodeling can be accomplished along with the garage to add still more inside space.

It is also possible to enclose a patio or terrace when extra space is at a premium; but this is really getting into the area of a true addition since most such areas are uncovered, and if they are covered, it is probably with framing and materials that are unsuitable for a true roof. Also, a patio or terrace may have a floor that is difficult to adapt for indoor use. If the patio has a properly framed roof (see p. 61) and a concrete base, it should be treated in the same way as a carport.

YOUR DETAILED PLANS

Once the preliminary ideas are sorted out and a tentative decision made as to what is to be done with the available space, it is time to get down to detailed planning. The first step is to make accurate measurements of the available area, noting all obstructions with some thought as to how to get around them. In the attic, decide how much headroom you want to leave, and run a plumb line down to the floor from the appropriate spot on the rafters. For a 6-foot sidewall, for example, measure out 6 feet on the plumb line and move it up the rafter until the point of the plumb bob touches the floor. That's the outside of your sidewall.

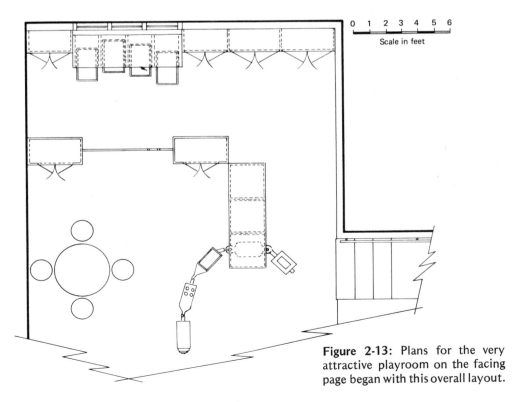

Scale in feet

Figure 2-13: Plans for the very attractive playroom on the facing page began with this overall layout.

Figure 2-14: Details for the playroom were then meticulously planned section by section.

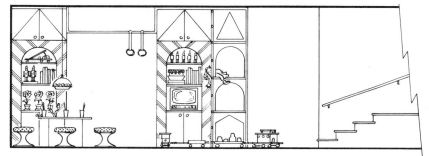

Figure 2-15: The playroom ready for children.

30

Built-ins are a natural for the kind of rooms made from extra space. Instead of walling off trouble spots, consider putting in some shelves or other storage facilities. Attic eaves, for example, can be made into drawers, closets, and other units. Use the area under the stairs or over the oil tank, instead of wasting it.

Make sure that you have provided for any heating, plus any plumbing and electrical lines (see Chapters 8 & 9), and have planned all partitions with standard sizes in lumber and finishing materials. Use standard sizes for doors and windows, making sure to allow for stops, trim, etc. All door and window sizes use the unframed dimensions. A 3'6"-wide door, for example, fits into an opening in the framing 3'6" wide. The door itself is closer to 3'4" wide.

You can't allow the proper wall widths if you don't know what materials you'll be using. Paneling, for example, is usually 1/4" thick, while gypsum wallboard is more than twice as thick (see Chapter 4). At any rate, you should visit your local building supply dealer early in the game to see what materials are available and at what cost. Choose materials that are functional, durable, and easily maintained.

You may find that the paneling you had in mind (Brazilian rosewood, for example) is much more expensive than you thought. There may be materials there that you didn't know existed, like some of the newer ceiling systems. Although changes can be made later, you should really have the entire room finished in your mind's eye before you even begin to draw plans. When decorating a recreation room, you might want to keep some kind of theme in mind (see pages 30 and 171-84).

This stage of planning should also consider amounts of materials needed. As you map out your partitions, determine where the studs will be and count them. Add in the top and bottom plates and other framing members as you go along. No doubt some of this will be altered once you actually get into it, but at least you'll have an idea as to how much you're talking about when it comes to pricing and ordering. Always add 5–10% over your estimate to allow for waste.

You should probably use 2 x 3 framing lumber for most of your partitions, or even 2 x 2s where you don't expect much stress. You won't need any 2 x 4s unless you have a bearing wall. If you're doing much other framing around doors and windows, 2 x 4s may be used just because they work better when doubled. (Two 2 x 3s set side by side are wider than a 2 x 3 on edge and will cause a bulge in the wall.) Remember, too, that "2 x 3" and "2 x 4" are the *nominal* dimensions (before drying and planing). The actual sizes are a half-inch smaller for most dimensions (see Table 4-1).

After the framing is up, the rest of the materials are a matter of taste. There is a wide variety of wall, ceiling, and floor coverings available from numerous manufacturers. The entire family should get together on the choices for these materials.

Spacing of studs has traditionally been 16″ o.c.—that is, there is normally a 16-inch span from the middle point of one stud to the middle of the next. For nonbearing partitions, however, 24″ centers are quite adequate. Furring strips are used to provide air space and nailing surface along basement walls and for ceiling tile. Use 1 x 2 or 1 x 3 lumber for furring strips, spaced according to the size of the material. For walls, 24″ centers are usual; most ceiling tiles are 12 x 12 inches and require furring strips at 12-inch intervals. Measure your own material before installing the furring.

USING A CONTRACTOR

Even if you plan on doing all the work yourself, it is a good idea to secure a couple of quotes from local contractors, if only to find out how much you'll save by doing it yourself. You may pick up some valuable ideas just from listening to them talk, and you may also want to get advice on the whole job, although you're just asking for quotes on a small part of it. Many contractors like to play teacher. One whom we know went into such detail that several of his customers decided to do the job themselves based on his instructions. On the other hand, you may find the contractors' quotes so reasonable that you may figure it isn't worth your while to do all the extra work yourself for the little money you'll save.

Call in the contractors or subcontractors at an early stage of the planning. Unless it's a really small job, always get three or more estimates from the most reliable firms you can find. It may not always be easy to pick out reputable contractors, but the Better Business Bureau should be able to at least steer you away from the worst ones. If you haven't had any experience with local contractors, friends or relatives are as good a source of information as any. Some areas have begun to license these firms to try and eliminate the real crooks. Check with the local authorities.

When requesting and comparing bids, make sure that each contractor specifies the same quality materials and guarantees the same amount of work to be done for each job. If and when you select a contractor or subcontractor(s), insist on a written agreement.

The contract should specifically indicate what work is to be performed, how it will be done, and how you will pay for it. It should provide for a method of determining extra charges for any changes that you request during the progress of the work. This is important to protect you from excessive extra charges, and a responsible contractor will also want to protect himself from losses through work having to be redone, and from misunderstanding and ill will through no fault of his own.

The contract should call for the contractor to obtain all needed permits and secure any necessary inspections and certificates as the work progresses. It should also provide that the contractor will be insured, as required by law, for workmen's compensation and for personal injury and property damage. And you may wish to ask for a performance bond, paid for by the contractor, to protect you in the event that he is unable for any reason to finish the job. Finally, specify in the contract that any debris from the job will be hauled away by the contractor.

Find out when the contractor will start the job and how long it will take him to complete it. If you are dealing with more than one contractor or subcontractor, you will have to coordinate their services. After the carpenter has framed the partitions, for example, the electrician and possibly the plumber will have to be called in to do their roughing-in before the walls are paneled.

Regarding payments to the contractor, make it a rule never to give any money for any home improvement project in advance. On a fairly large job, the contractor will want partial payments during the course of the work—for example, one-third when the job is half completed, one-third on completion, and the balance when all necessary certificates are obtained. Some homeowners want the right to withhold a part of the payment for a period of time, usually two to three months, to give them a chance to live with the job and make sure that everything is in good working order.

Many handy homeowners prefer to have a contractor do a part of the job while supplying the finishing touches themselves. You may wish to have a carpenter do all the roughing-in—furring the walls, framing the partitions, etc.—and then install the paneling, ceiling tiles, and floor yourself. Or you may have the carpenter do the paneling and then take over making the built-in cabinets, bar, and other refinements. In any event, you should probably have such things as plumbing and electrical work professionally done. Perhaps you can work along with these tradesmen if you so choose—boring holes and pulling wires for the electrician while he makes the

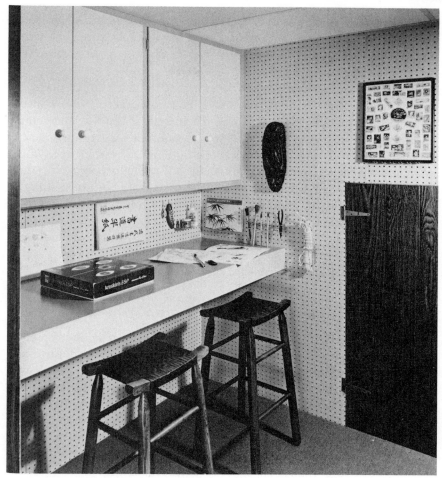

Figure 2-16: This hobby center was part of an extensive remodeling job that was roughed in by a carpenter and finished by a dedicated do-it-yourselfer (*courtesy of Masonite Corporation*).

connections and installs the fixtures, or doing the relatively simple task of tying into existing water lines for new supply lines to a basement bathroom, while leaving the more complex work of connecting the waste lines to the professional plumber.

Whatever you decide to do, make sure that all the agreed-upon conditions are clearly spelled out in the contracts that you draw up with the various tradesmen so there can be no misunderstanding as to who is responsible for what. And see that you live up to your end of the agreement, doing whatever must be done in good time so that you don't cause unnecessary delays for the contractors.

Time is money to them, and if they are forced to wait for you to do your job, it's cash out of their pockets. You can be sure they won't be so willing to work along with you next time you undertake a home improvement project.

The time of year when you contract to have the job done can mean quite a difference in the cost. To a contractor who concentrates on remodeling and finishing off interiors, the fall and winter months are busy times, while spring and summer are slack seasons. If he has a good crew of workers, he would much rather keep them busy during these slack months than lay them off and risk their finding other jobs before business picks up again. So he is willing to cut into his profit margin to keep these men on his payroll. Consequently, the homeowner who schedules a project for these off-seasons reaps the benefit. But again be sure that your contract spells out the type of materials and workmanship that you want. Don't settle for a bargain job that sacrifices quality.

FINANCING THE JOB

Whether you agree to a contractor's bid on your project or whether you have estimated material requirements and determined the cost of doing it yourself, you now know how much money it will take to do the job. The next question is how you are going to pay for it. The answer, in this day and age, should be obvious—you'll finance it. And you'll probably find lending institutions in your locale that will be more than happy to finance your improvement, for most consider such a loan a solid investment.

There are many types of credit organizations that are in business to help you finance your projects (and, of course, to make a reasonable profit along the way). Once you have determined how much you will need for your project, shop around to find the one that best suits your requirements.

Bank Loan

Before the bank will talk to you, you'll have to provide them with at least a rough idea of what it is they're being asked to pay for. The best way is to bring in a rough sketch and an estimate from a contractor, whether you use him or not. (This is another good reason for having the contractor make an estimate, even if you do it yourself.) Before you get any ideas, don't expect to have the bank loan you the money including the contractor's price and then do the work yourself, pocketing the difference. The bank may decide to pay the contractor directly and will want proof of what work has been done in any case. Bank rates and conditions vary throughout the nation.

Life Insurance Loan

You don't necessarily have to go to the bank. One alternative is cash, if you're one of those people who has enough to spare. Another, and the best way of all, is to borrow on the cash value of your life insurance. It's still possible to borrow up to 95% of the value at a very low interest rate—perhaps as low as 5%. Contact your insurance agent for current cash value, rates, etc.

FHA Loan

The Federal Housing Authority (FHA), now an arm of the Department of Housing and Urban Development (HUD), has two types of loans for home improvement, but the *long-term* type applies only to structural changes such as additions. Since the improvements described here are ordinarily not in that category, we will discuss only *Title I* loans. Title I loans are designed for alterations or repairs that "enhance the basic livability" of the home, which should apply to most of the projects described in this book. These loans are made through regular lending institutions and are insured by the FHA. The limit is $5,000, with up to seven years to pay. The interest rate varies with the money market, but is lower than conventional rates. In times of tight money, however, these loans tend to dry up completely.

"Open-End" Mortgage

You may be able to use your current mortgage to borrow more money if it has an "open-end" provision. If you've made payments on your home for several years, you may be able to borrow an amount that will bring the principal back up to its original sum. If your mortgage was for $25,000, for example, and you've brought it down to $22,000, you may be able to borrow the $3,000 back again—perhaps at the original rate. Check with your lawyer or the bank on this.

Refinanced Mortgage

If you don't have an open-end mortgage, perhaps you can refinance your present indebtedness. This may be a poor financial deal, forcing you to abandon a low-interest mortgage for a high one, but it could also be the only way to get extra cash in hard times.

38   Usually it will be greatest along the lower parts of the wall. Like leakage, seepage is caused by excessive water pressure on the outside of the basement walls. It may also be due to capillary action, which draws water from the moist soil through porous sections of the masonry.

Condensation looks very much like seepage, but here the moisture comes from air inside the basement, not from water outside the walls (although seepage from outside may be a factor in creating the conditions causing condensation). Condensation usually occurs during warm, humid weather when the cool masonry walls seem to "sweat." It can also occur during colder months when warm air is discharged by a clothes dryer or similar appliance; moisture from this air collects on the cooler walls in the form of droplets, which may be mistaken for seepage from outside.

There is a simple test to determine whether a damp wall is the result of seepage or condensation. Tape a small mirror or a piece of sheet metal to the wall (or use a waterproof mastic if the wall is too wet for tape to stick). Leave it there overnight and inspect it the next day. If the surface of the mirror is fogged or the sheet metal is damp, the moisture came from inside the basement, indicating that condensation is to blame. If the surface of the mirror or sheet metal is dry and clear while the surrounding wall is damp, seepage is the problem.

Figure 3-1: You can imagine what a foundation leak would do to a handsome basement room like this—and to the family's musical future.

CONDENSATION CURES

If condensation is the cause of your moisture miseries, the remedy is to dry out the air in the basement as much as possible.

Adequate ventilation is essential for a dry basement. In cool, dry weather, keep the basement windows open whenever possible. On hot, humid days, keep them closed; warm, moist air may even cause mildew to form on the cooler masonry walls. If your basement has too few windows to provide needed ventilation, a small exhaust fan installed in a window or ducted to the outside will help.

Pipes that tend to sweat in hot weather should be wrapped with insulation. This is especially important if finishing off the basement ceiling is part of your plans. Otherwise, moisture dripping from the pipes will ruin your ceiling tiles or panels.

Clothes dryers should always be vented to the outside. This is a relatively easy do-it-yourself job. The vent pipe is normally run through a hole in the header joist or stringer joist (these are the joists that rest on the sills, which in turn are bolted to the top of the foundation walls). The hole can be cut either from inside the basement or, with careful measurements, from outside; its diameter will depend on the size of the vent port on your dryer. First drill a 1/2" pilot hole; then use either a saber or keyhole saw to cut the hole. Insert a hooded fitting through the hole from the outside; then connect the dryer's exhaust port to this fitting with flexible pipe. Both the fitting and the flexible pipe can be purchased at most hardware stores.

Figure 3-2: Flexible hose helps when a dryer must be vented through the maze of wire and pipes, typical of many basements. This vent cuts down greatly on basement condensation.

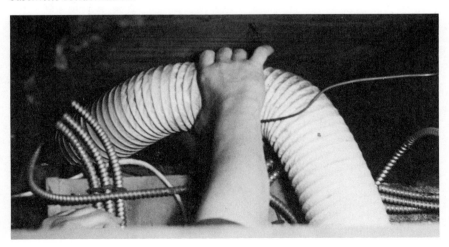

If you do not have a clothes dryer, try to avoid hanging clothes to dry in the basement. The moisture from the clothes will enter the air and show up as condensation on the walls.

Where basement condensation persists, an electric dehumidifier or chemical drying agents may be needed to remove moisture from the air and keep your basement dry.

Condensation Problems in New Houses

If you are one of the fortunate few who have been able to move into a brand new house in this time of skyrocketing costs and hard-to-obtain mortgages, chances are your condensation problems are greater than most. Condensation is at its maximum in new houses. During construction, literally tons of water are used—in concrete, mortar, plaster, wallpaper paste, tile work, and even some types of paint. This water gradually evaporates, giving a higher moisture content than normal to air throughout the house and ending up as condensation on basement walls and on windows in every room.

All the steps described above (especially providing adequate ventilation) should be employed to assist this normal drying-out process. In addition, be patient. Do not try to accelerate the process by turning up the furnace to extremely high temperatures. This will only cause uneven drying, exaggerating the effects of normal material shrinkage and almost surely resulting in greater patch-and-repair problems later on.

Controlling Seepage

If seepage is the cause of your basement dampness, a simple coat of paint may be the solution. Not just any paint, but one that is resistant to water, alkali, and mildew, and also adheres well to concrete. This will provide a watertight coating that is both durable and decorative.

Most such paints can be applied to damp and uncured concrete as well as to previously painted surfaces. As with any paint job, the key to success is careful preparation.

Unpainted concrete, whether new or old, must be clean before application of the paint. Grease, oil, and dirt should be removed with a strong cleaning agent such as trisodium phosphate. After scrubbing with a stiff-bristled brush, rinse the surface thoroughly with water to remove all residue. Allow the walls to dry for 24 hours.

Figure 3-3: A coat of mildew- and water-resistant paint, especially formulated for application to the foundation, will help control seepage.

On a previously painted wall, all paint that is flaking, blistering, cracking, or chalking must be removed. This is done by scraping and brushing with a wire brush. Chemical removers can also be used. As with new concrete, the surface should then be scrubbed clean, rinsed, and allowed to dry.

If the walls are whitewashed, scrub them with a dilute mixture of muriatic acid (10 parts water to 1 part acid). Wear rubber gloves for this job, and be careful not to splash any of the mixture on your skin or in your eyes. (If you do, rinse immediately with plenty of water.) Again, rinse the surface thoroughly after scrubbing and allow it to dry.

Before painting, patch large cracks and holes in the concrete, following the directions given on page 42 for plugging leaks. Hairline cracks and pores or pinholes need not be filled. The full-bodied paint will cover them.

Apply the paint with a brush or roller, covering the surface

42 evenly and thoroughly. Normally, a single coat will do the job. But if the concrete or concrete block is very porous, a second coat may be required.

A more serious seepage problem suggests a structural fault that will probably have to be corrected from outside the wall. You may prefer to leave this project to the professionals since it involves excavating a trench wide enough to allow working space and deep enough to reach the problem area. That's a lot of digging. The masonry surface must then be scrubbed clean before a coating of cement plaster is troweled on. This is followed by a second coating and, finally, a coating of asphalt cement or plastic sealer.

Where excessive subsoil moisture is causing the seepage problem, drain tile should be laid around the foundation footings to carry water away from the house—another digging project. Tiles should be pitched downward 1/4-inch per foot toward the drainage point. Joints between tiles should be covered with strips of tarpaper to keep out dirt, and the tiles should both rest on and be covered by a layer of gravel or crushed stone.

PLUGGING LEAKS

Wall Leaks

When water is trickling through the basement wall, your first step is to plug the leak. This is best done with a quick-setting hydraulic cement that can be applied even when a crack is under pressure—that is, when water is pouring through it. Apply the cement with a trowel or wide-bladed putty knife, holding the cement in place until the flow of water is stopped.

Such patches are usually only temporary and should be replaced when the crack is dry. For a normal, dry repair, first chisel out the crack to form an inverted V-groove, about 1/2-inch wide at the surface and wider beneath so that the patching material will be locked in place. (Your dentist uses a similar technique when filling your teeth.) Use a cold chisel and a mash (stone hammer) or ball peen hammer to undercut the crack. (Your claw hammer should be reserved for carpentry and woodworking projects.) Clean away all loose rubble and dust, and clean with a wire brush. Flush with water to remove all dust particles.

Mix together 1 part cement to 2-1/2 parts of clean sand. Add enough water to make a stiff mixture, making sure to wet all parts of the sand–cement. Dampen the area to be patched; then force the

Figure 3-4: For permanent repair, chisel out the crack in an inverted "V" (about 1/2 inch at the surface, wider underneath). Use a cold chisel and heavy hammer, and always wear safety goggles or glasses. Fill with patching cement.

mixture into the crack with a trowel, filling it completely. Keep the patched area slightly damp for a few days to allow the cement to cure thoroughly. If that doesn't solve your leakage problem, you will probably have to attack it from the outside, as described above for seepage.

In a concrete block foundation wall, water may leak through a defective mortar joint between blocks. To repair this, first scrape away all loose and crumbling mortar, using a cold chisel or an old

44 screwdriver. Clean out the joint with a wire brush, and rinse with water to remove all dust particles. Make a mortar mix of 1 part masonry cement to 3 parts clean, dry sand. Then add enough water to make a workable, but fairly stiff, mixture. Force the mortar into the joint with a trowel, striking it off flush with the surface of the block. Allow the mortar to dry thoroughly.

Leaks at the wall–floor joint can be similarly corrected with cement. Even more effective is a two-part epoxy resin compound that forms an effective seal against hydrostatic pressure at this point. Once again, the area should be thoroughly cleaned before making the repair. The epoxy material is mixed immediately before use and brushed or troweled into place. Two coats are usually recommended.

Floor Leaks

Leaks in concrete floors are repaired in the same way as wall leaks: undercutting, cleaning, and patching with a sand–cement mixture. However, floor leaks may be indicative of more serious

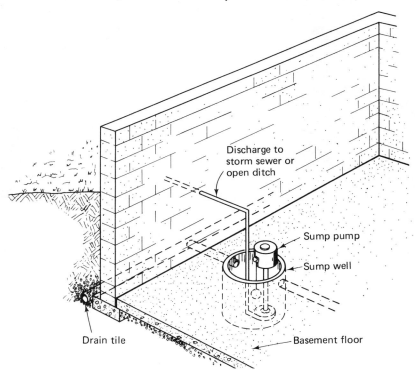

Discharge to storm sewer or open ditch

Sump pump

Sump well

Drain tile

Basement floor

Figure 3-5: Where there is no natural gravity outlet, a sump pump will help carry the water up to empty into a natural outlet. However, a basement that needs such drainage might be a poor place to build living space.

problems. Your home may be in a very low, wet location, or it may be built over a marshy area or an underground stream. In that case, a drainage tile system may have to be installed, as described above for major seepage problems. Sometimes not even that works. Where there is no natural gravity outlet, a sump pump can be installed in an unused part of the basement. If a home has been built on a poorly drained site and nothing seems to help, you'll probably have to abandon any plans for finishing the basement.

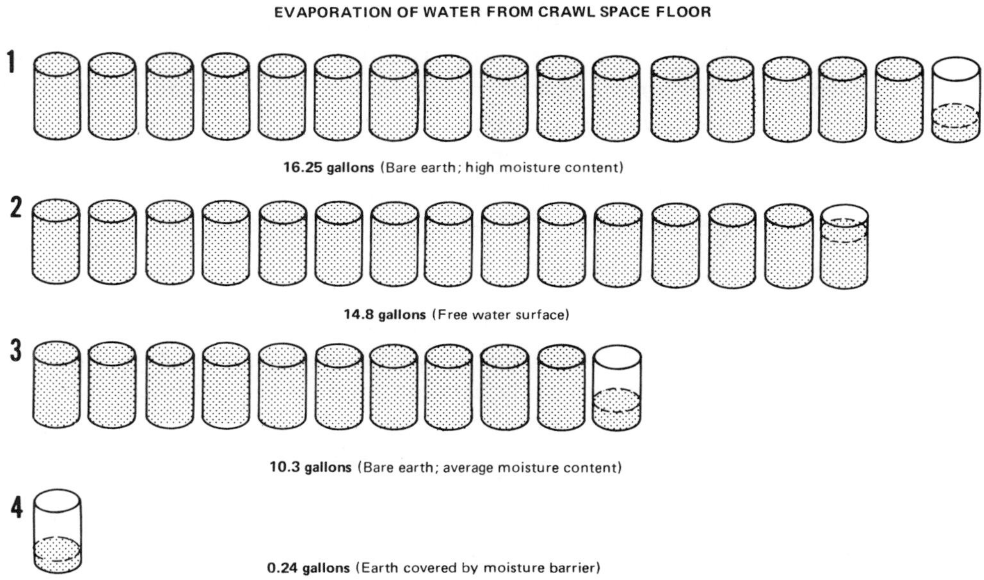

EVAPORATION OF WATER FROM CRAWL SPACE FLOOR

16.25 gallons (Bare earth; high moisture content)

14.8 gallons (Free water surface)

10.3 gallons (Bare earth; average moisture content)

0.24 gallons (Earth covered by moisture barrier)

Figure 3-6: Graph above illustrates how the earth under a crawl space can contain more moisture than an open water surface. Note the great improvement obtained with the use of a moisture barrier (No. 4).

CRAWL SPACE PROBLEMS

Crawl spaces present some special problems because cold and dampness commonly invade these areas. Occasionally, unpleasant odors result. These conditions make living on the floor above somewhat less than ideal. The conditions, thankfully, are usually curable.

Again, adequate ventilation is essential. There should be vents or louvers on at least two opposite sides of the crawl space to provide cross-ventilation. If necessary, you can install vents by cutting holes through the header joists (similar to installing a dryer vent, described

46 previously). If the foundation is of concrete block, simply knock out a block and replace it with a vent. Louvered vents, which can be closed off in damp or cold weather, are best. They should also be screened to keep out rodents and other small animals.

Cold floors in rooms over crawl spaces present another problem. The best solution is to install 4″ insulation batts between the floor joists. Staple the batts to the bottom of the joists, forming an air space between the subfloor and the insulation. Staple a vapor barrier of heavy felt paper below the insulation to seal out any moisture. Make sure that the entire area beneath the floor is covered.

If dampness persists, cover the ground in the crawl space with tarpaper. Overlap the joints 3 to 4 inches, and seal the tarpaper to the foundation walls with asphalt compound. Then spread a 2″ layer of dry sand over the tarpaper. This should ensure that the area above the crawl space will be cozy and dry year round.

PREVENTIVE MEASURES

Patching holes and cracks and waterproofing basement walls solve the immediate problems of leakage and seepage. But since the ultimate cause is excess water accumulation in the ground around the foundation walls, this situation should also be corrected diverting surface water before it can come into contact with the foundation.

Check gutters and downspouts for leaks or improper pitch that may cause water to collect along the foundation wall. Gutters that are clogged with leaves and other debris may also divert water onto the ground alongside the house and, eventually, into the basement. Downspouts should be connected to a storm sewer or to an underground dry well located at least 10 feet away from the foundation. Downspouts not so connected should empty onto a concrete splash block that carries the water runoff away from the house walls.

To carry away rainwater as quickly as possible, the ground surface should slope away sharply at foundation walls, then more gradually to at least 10 feet from the walls. If such is not the case, fill in around the foundation with new soil, taking special care in areas where puddles form during rainy weather. Tamp the soil firmly, and sow it with good grass seed or cover it with sod rolled down evenly and firmly. If the new grading extends above basement windows, protect these with curved metal shells or concrete walls. Gravel in the bottom of these protected areas will facilitate drainage. Hinged plastic covers may be installed to admit light but keep out rain and snow.

Figure 3-7: A splash block will help carry water away from the foundation when downspouts are not connected to sewers.

Where concrete walks or driveways are adjacent to the foundation wall, they should also slope away gradually. The walk–wall joint should be concave or sharply angled to keep out water.

If joints are not so protected, or if they are broken or otherwise damaged, the defects should be corrected. Chip away loose or damaged concrete. Scrub both the wall and the walk clean, and roughen both surfaces with a cold chisel. You can then apply an epoxy resin compound to the joint, as described above for basement wall–floor joints. Or you can use a mixture of one part cement to 2-1/2 parts sand. Moisten the concrete surfaces; then trowel the cement–sand mixture into the joint, sloping it sharply away from the foundation wall for at least two inches. To build up the portion of the walk next to the foundation without chipping out present concrete, use a vinyl patching concrete which can be "feathered" at the edges.

48   ## BEWARE OF "MIRACLE CURES"

If all else fails and you must call in a professional to try to solve your basement dampness problem, exercise a degree of caution, and beware of "miracle cures." There are many highly reputable firms in the basement waterproofing business, but there are also some of lesser repute. Follow the usual practice of checking with the local Better Business Bureau, consumer protection groups, and other homeowners who have dealt with the firm before you sign any contract.

The Basics of Framework

4

Most remodeling projects will include the building of walls and partitions, and behind every good wall there must be a good frame. When finishing off a basement, an attic, a garage, or a breezeway, you are not likely to have to build any load-bearing walls—those that provide structural support for other parts of the house. The purpose of your framing is to provide both a sturdy backing for the wall-finishing material (wallboard, paneling, or whatever) and a complex of gluing or nailing surfaces to which that material can be fastened.

With that concept firmly in mind, you will avoid many of the common mistakes often made by the novice carpenter. Two of the most frequent framing sins are: (1) Spacing framing members improperly so that they do not provide backing for wallboard edges or else require excessive cutting of wallboard, and (2) failing to provide backing at corners. With a little care and planning, they won't be committed on your job. The basic principles of good framing are easy to learn and to follow.

For your home improvement projects, all partitions are built in basically the same way—with some slight differences. In the basement, for example, you will probably be building on a concrete floor that is uneven or pitched for drainage. In an attic with a sloping roof, you will be building short "knee" walls. But in all cases the purpose of the framing is the same: to provide a backing for the finished wall. Let's start with a typical basement framing job.

50   FRAMING THE BASEMENT ROOM

None of the basement partitions will be load-bearing, so 2 x 3 lumber can be used for the framing in most cases. An exception would be that rare basement that is extremely high, where 2 x 4s might be needed for greater stability. Another exception is a partition that is located directly beneath a wood beam or a steel I-beam. Since this partition will enclose one or more supporting columns (usually 3 or 4 inches in diameter), 2 x 4s or even wider lumber is preferred to accommodate the width of the columns and the beam while maintaining an unbroken line. Of course, if this partition is to be finished on only one side, the narrower lumber could be used, with the framing kept flush with the beam and columns on that side.

Utility grade lumber is fine for framing purposes. At the lumberyard, select pieces that are as straight as possible for use as *plates* (horizontal framing members at the top and bottom of a wall) and *studs* (vertical framing members).

Studs are normally spaced 16″ o.c. for load-bearing walls, but for our purposes, 24″ spacing is usually acceptable—and also cheaper and quicker to build. Some types of thin wall paneling, however, require backing at 16″ intervals. Follow the stud-spacing recommendations of the manufacturer of the wall-finishing material you intend to install.

Carefully measure and snap a chalk line on the basement floor where one edge of the partition is to be located. Select a straight piece of lumber for the *soleplate* (bottom), and secure it to the floor. Use 12d common nails on a wood floor (not too likely in the basement), helical concrete nails on a concrete floor. Concrete nails must be driven perfectly straight or they will bend and may snap off—for this reason, it is strongly recommended that you wear safety glasses during this operation. If the concrete is too hard for nailing, you can make holes, using an electric drill with a masonry bit, and then insert lead anchors into the holes and fasten the plate with lag screws. The soleplate should run the full length of the partition, including those areas where doorways will be located. But do not nail or lag the door sections—they will be cut out later.

Select another straight piece of lumber for the *top plate*, and lay it on the floor alongside the secured soleplate. Stud locations will be marked simultaneously on both plates. This both insures accuracy and saves you the bother of making duplicate measurements.

If your partition begins at a masonry wall that is to be finished off, allow for the thickness of furring strips (usually 3/4″)

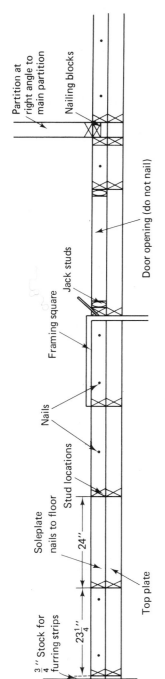

Figure 4-1: Laying out a partition for the basement. The sole plate is fastened to the floor, then the top plate is laid alongside, and both are marked at the same time.

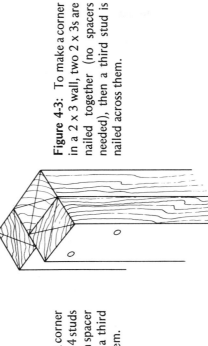

Figure 4-3: To make a corner in a 2 x 3 wall, two 2 x 3s are nailed together (no spacers needed), then a third stud is nailed across them.

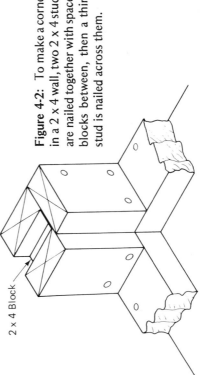

Figure 4-2: To make a corner in a 2 x 4 wall, two 2 x 4 studs are nailed together with spacer blocks between, then a third stud is nailed across them.

on that wall before marking the position of the first stud. Place a framing square across both plates, and mark a pencil line along the blade of the square. Mark an "**X**" on each plate on the side of the line where the stud is to be located.

The center point of the next stud should be 24" from the outside edge of the corner stud (or 16", if your partition calls for 16" centers). Therefore, the edge of the second stud will be 23-1/4" (or 15-1/4") from the edge of the corner stud. Measure this distance, and mark a second line with **X**s alongside to indicate the location of the second stud.

Locations for the remaining studs are determined simply by holding the 24" (or the 16") blade of the framing square along the plates with the end at the mark of the last stud, and then marking the location of the next. Make sure you mark the **X**s on the same side of the line—ahead of the square—each time.

MEASURING TIPS: Keep your pencil sharp. An error of 1/16" or 1/8" at each stud caused by marking with a dull pencil will be compounded considerably along the length of a sizable partition, and will cause unnecessary difficulties when the time comes to install paneling or wallboard over the framing.

Laying Out Doors and Partitions

When you are planning the layout of your room, it is best to locate doorways in the partitions at intervals that will require the least cutting and fitting of paneling materials, if this is possible. Locations of doors are marked on the plates after you have marked all the stud locations. Measure out the door width on the plates, add 1 inch on each side for the door jamb, and then mark on each side the locations of the *jack studs* that will frame the doorway. (Jack studs are shorter than full-length studs and serve to support that part of the wall framing above the door opening.) Full-length studs will be required alongside the jack studs if regularly spaced studs do not fall there—mark these positions as well.

Where a second partition is to meet the main partition at right angles, forming a "**T**," it is necessary to provide studs at either side for nailing purposes. For added sturdiness, fasten short nailing blocks between these two flanking studs, and secure the corner stud of the second partition to these blocks.

A corner is usually formed by nailing two studs together with blocks between, and then adding a third across these two. (For a 2 x 3 wall, no blocks are needed.) If the inside of the partition is to be left unfinished, as in a storage area, you can simply use two studs joined in an "**L**".

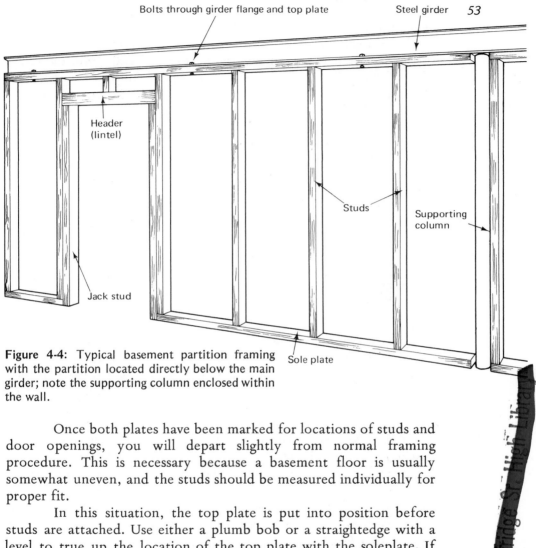

Bolts through girder flange and top plate

Steel girder

Header (lintel)

Studs

Supporting column

Jack stud

Sole plate

Figure 4-4: Typical basement partition framing with the partition located directly below the main girder; note the supporting column enclosed within the wall.

Once both plates have been marked for locations of studs and door openings, you will depart slightly from normal framing procedure. This is necessary because a basement floor is usually somewhat uneven, and the studs should be measured individually for proper fit.

In this situation, the top plate is put into position before studs are attached. Use either a plumb bob or a straightedge with a level to true up the location of the top plate with the soleplate. If the partition is running at right angles to the ceiling joists, simply nail the top plate to each joist. If the partition is running directly beneath a steel girder, you must drill holes through the top plate and the girder, and fasten them together with bolts. If the partition is running in the same direction as the joists, you will face one of the following situations.

The partition may be directly beneath a joist. In this case, simply nail the top plate to the joist with 12d nails. However, you must also provide a nailing surface for ceiling material or ceiling furring strips. This is accomplished by fastening nailers to each side

54   of the joist flush with the bottom of the joist. Use 1″ or 2″ lumber, depending on the amount of nailing face needed.

The partition may also fall somewhere between two joists. In this case, fasten headers between the joists, 1-1/2″ from the lower edge of the joists. Then nail a 2 x 6 along the full top length of the plate to provide corner nailing surfaces for the ceiling material. Fasten this assembly to the headers with 12d common nails.

Figure 4-5: When a partition is parallel to, but between, joists, first fasten headers between joists, then secure partition plate to nailer board.

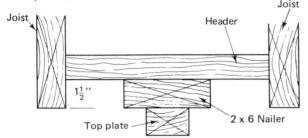

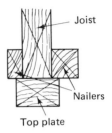

Figure 4-6: When a basement partition is directly below a joist, nailers must be provided for ceiling material.

With both top and soleplates in position, measure and cut studs to fit snugly between the plates. Use 8d nails to toenail the studs on all four sides to both plates. You will find it easier to nail the narrow edges first, front and back. *One exception*: The studs flanking the door openings should be nailed only on the narrow edges and away from the opening—do not nail in the direction where the plate is to be cut. This can prove disastrous for a sharp saw when you cut away this plate later.

When all full-length studs are in place, cut the plates at the door openings, alongside the studs. Cut two jack studs the height of the door plus 1-1/4″ to allow for the top frame and door clearance. Nail these studs to the full-length flanking studs and to the soleplate.

The *lintel*, or *header*, over the door opening of a 2 x 4 partition is formed by nailing together two 2 x 4s and setting them atop the short jack studs with their narrow dimensions vertical. Since the 2 x 4s together total only 3 inches, you will have to sandwich 1/2″ plywood spacers to keep the sides flush with the studs. For a 2 x 3 partition, however, two 2 x 3s would be too wide—the 3″ dimension is actually 2-1/2 inches. Use a single 2 x 4 and nail a 1 x 4 to it, with spacers of 1/4″ plywood between to make the header the same width as the wall framing. Set the lintel in place on top of the jack studs, and nail through the full-length studs. A short stud, called a *cripple stud*, is then fastened between the header and the top plate. (See Table 4-1 on page 62 for exact lumber sizes.)

Figure 4-7: Studs are toenailed to the floor plate, with nails driven into sides and edges.

Figure 4-8: After studs are secured to the floor plate, they are checked for plumb (perfectly vertical) with a carpenter's level.

Figure 4-9: With studs plumb, they are toenailed to top plate. Note how plate is cut around pipe in ceiling.

Window and Pass-Through Openings

Openings that do not reach the floor—a window or pass-through, for example—are framed in similar fashion. Regularly spaced short studs and jack studs support a flat 2 x 3 or 2 x 4 sill; then a header across the top rests on jack studs on the sill.

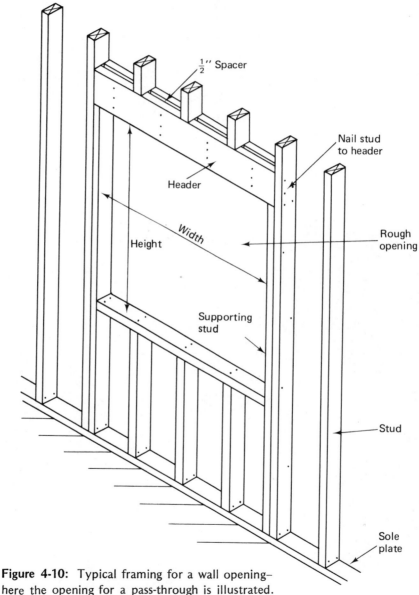

Figure 4-10: Typical framing for a wall opening—here the opening for a pass-through is illustrated. Door framing is similarly constructed.

Concealing Obstructions

Obstructions such as meter boxes, soil stacks, and very low-hanging pipes are concealed by building box frames around them, attaching the box frames to walls and joists. While the structure will, of course, vary to conform to the individual obstruction, the important consideration is to provide a solid nailing surface for the material that will be used to finish off the box—usually the same paneling that is used in the rest of the room. Meters and valves must be provided with access doors. These may be fashioned of plywood covered with paneling material.

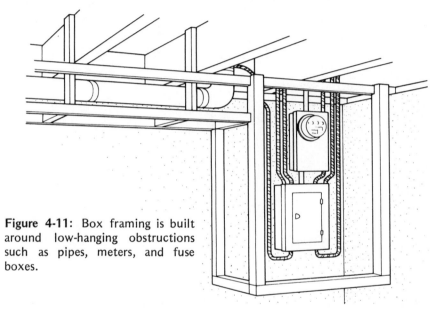

Figure 4-11: Box framing is built around low-hanging obstructions such as pipes, meters, and fuse boxes.

Covering the Walls

On masonry walls, fasten furring strips (1 x 2s or 1 x 3s) horizontally or vertically, depending on the type of wall covering you will use. Check each furring strip with a level and use shims where necessary to assure a plumb wall. You can check for evenness by holding a long straightedge across the faces of several strips.

There are several methods for fastening furring strips to masonry walls. Helical concrete nails are one possibility. Certain adhesives can be used to attach the strips directly to some types of masonry walls. Or you can use anchor plates, flat perforated plates with nails protruding from their faces. These plates are fastened to the masonry with a special adhesive. Furring strips are then hammered onto the nails, and the nail points are bent over into the

Figure 4-12: Attach furring strips to masonry walls with special hardened nails. They must be driven straight and hard with a hammer. Even with these precautions, they sometimes snap off (a good reason for wearing safety glasses and, if it's available, a hard hat as well).

wood. Another method is to drill holes into the masonry, insert plugs or expansion shields, and secure the furring strips either with wood screws driven into the plugs or with fasteners driven into the expansion shields.

Furring strips are also used to frame around basement windows. You can frame the inside of the window recess and extend your wall covering into this space, if there is sufficient clearance at the sides so that a window may still be opened.

Before applying paneling to the exterior walls, staple a layer of polyethylene plastic sheeting over the furring strips as an added precaution against dampness.

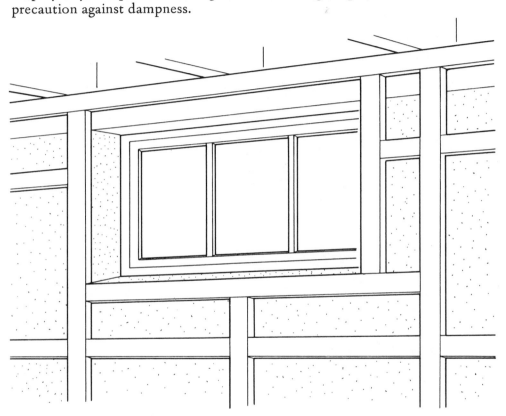

Figure 4-13: Use furring strips to make framing around basement windows so that paneling or other wall covering can be fastened properly.

Finishing the Ceiling

The ceiling of your basement room may be applied directly to the joists. If there are a number of pipes suspended directly below the joists, it may be best to fur the entire ceiling to conceal these obstructions. And if you plan to use tiles for the ceiling, you will have to install furring strips to accommodate the width of the tiles—usually in 12″ modules (see Chapter 6).

60 FRAMING THE ATTIC ROOM

General rules for framing an attic room are similar to those just outlined—with a few important variations.

Most attic rooms have sloping ceilings following the roof line. When constructing a partition along this line, it is generally best to secure the soleplate, and then fasten short dwarf studs alongside each rafter. These will usually be 16″ o.c., except in very old houses.

Figure 4-14: Attic framing is slightly different in construction from basement framing. The knee walls (short studs between plates and rafters) and collar beams also serve as ceiling joists for the ceiling.

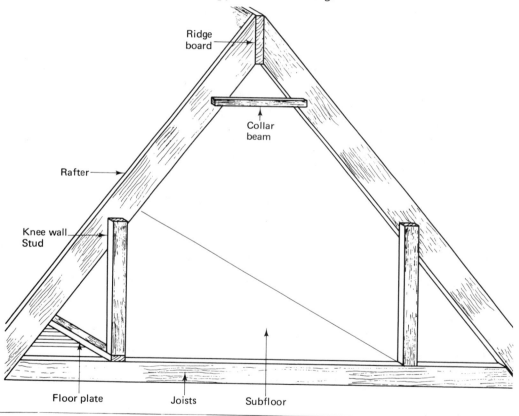

A simple way to do this is to first fasten studs at each end, using a level to ensure that they are plumb. Then snap a chalk line between these two across all the rafters. This allows you to properly line up each short stud. Check with a straightedge after each few studs are installed to make sure that a straight wall line is being maintained.

Use Beams as Joists

The attic should have "collar" beams overhead, holding the rafters together and usually spaced on every third set of rafters. If these are level (as they should be), they can serve as ceiling joists for the room. Simply install similar beams between the rafters where they are missing. Again, a line and straightedge will ensure your keeping them level and maintaining a smooth ceiling line.

Figure 4-15: Whenever possible, build wall framing on the floor and then tilt it up into position. This convenient method is often used if a breezeway or carport is being enclosed.

When constructing a full-height partition, you will find another difference from basement framing. This occurs after you have marked both plates. Unlike a basement, where an uneven floor must be assumed, it is possible to cut the studs and fasten them to the top plate before securing the plate in its final position, greatly simplifying the procedure.

Measure the exact length of the studs, and then cut them to size. Set the top plate on edge in an area of the floor where you have room to lay out the studs to full length below it. Carefully line up each stud with the mark on the top plate. (Remember that the stud should be on the **X** side of the mark.) Nail through the plate into the stud, using two 12d nails on each stud.

When the entire length of the partition has been assembled in this manner, lift it into place on the soleplate. Fasten a few studs to the soleplate by toenailing with 8d nails; then plumb the partition and secure the top plate using the same methods detailed for basement construction. Then complete the nailing of all studs to the soleplate.

62 FRAMING GARAGES, PORCHES, AND BREEZEWAYS

The partitions for garages, porches, and breezeways are framed in essentially the same way as those in basements. In a garage, three of the walls are already framed—a distinct advantage. You should always use 2 x 4s for any outside walls.

Where there isn't a finished ceiling already in place, the easiest way to build a wall is on its side, somewhat as described under attic framing above. Instead of first nailing the soleplate on the floor, build the entire frame on its side; then raise it into place, and nail it to the floor. The reason you can't do this when there is a finished ceiling is that you can't tip it into place without damaging the ceiling.

Table 4-1: ACTUAL DIMENSIONS OF LUMBER IN INCHES			
NOMINAL SIZE	*DRESSED SIZE*	*NOMINAL SIZE*	*DRESSED SIZE*
1 x 1	3/4" x 3/4"	2 x 2	1-1/2" x 1-1/2"
1 x 2	3/4" x 1-1/2"	2 x 3	1-1/2" x 2-1/2"
1 x 4	3/4" x 3-1/2"	2 x 4	1-1/2" x 3-1/2"
1 x 6	3/4" x 5-1/2"	2 x 6	1-1/2" x 5-1/2"
1 x 8	3/4" x 7-1/4"	2 x 8	1-1/2" x 7-1/4"
1 x 10	3/4" x 9-1/4"	2 x 10	1-1/2" x 9-1/4"
1 x 12	3/4" x 11-1/4"	2 x 12	1-1/2" x 11-1/4"

Insulation for the New Space

5

In these days of high energy costs, proper insulation is even more important than it always has been. Insulating walls and ceilings that have contact with the outside will help keep your newfound living space comfortably warm in winter and cool in summer. The insulation acts as a barrier to heat, no matter which way the heat is traveling.

TYPES OF INSULATION

Thermal insulation (that designed to retard the transfer of heat) comes in four basic types.

Loose Fill

This consists of material such as mineral wool, vermiculite, expanded mica, or cellulose fiber. It comes in bags and is poured in place between joists or blown into position between studs, using special equipment. This latter application is fine if you live in an older house that has no insulation in the walls, but it is best left to the professionals who have the expensive blowers and other equipment needed to do the job.

Rigid Boards

Rigid insulation boards are made of relatively dense foamed glass or foamed plastic. They come in a wide range of sizes and are attached directly to wall studs, either as an exterior sheathing or as a finished interior wall. Since it is somewhat soft and dents and scratches easily, it is advisable to protect it on inside walls with a chair-height wainscoting.

Figure 5-1: Insulation batts (here fiberglass) are stapled between the studs. A stapling gun or stapling hammer is the right tool for the job (*courtesy of Johns-Manville*).

Blankets or Batts

These are normally made of mineral wool or fiberglass encased in paper. On one side, the paper is asphalt-impregnated or otherwise treated to prevent moisture from seeping into the insulation and causing it to rot. Blanket insulation comes in rolls up

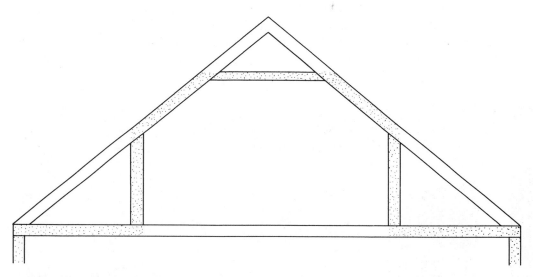

Figure 5-2: This illustration diagrams the correct placement of insulation (shaded area) in a finished-off attic. Such insulation is a must for efficient and economical space conditioning since it prevents heat loss in the winter and heat gain in the summer.

to 50 feet long; batts are usually 48 inches in length. Both types come in various thicknesses and in widths to fit between studs, joists, and rafters. They are commonly held in place with staples and are installed easily and speedily.

Reflective Insulation

This consists of a metal foil, usually aluminum, that turns back heat by reflection rather than by the thickness of the material, as with other types of insulation. It must be installed with the bright side facing an air space of at least 3/4 inch. The metal foil is available in both flat and accordion-fold form; the latter is somewhat easier to install.

THE EFFICIENCY FACTOR

Most manufacturers rate the insulating efficiency of their products by one of two systems. The more common involves an **R** number, indicating the amount of resistance to heat. If two types of installation are applicable to your situation and are equally priced, the one with the higher R number would be preferable.

A second rating system considers the amount of heat that will pass through a product under known conditions, expressed as a **C** or a **U** number. A low C or U number indicates that only a small amount of heat can get through, therefore, the lower the number, the better.

Figure 5-3: A completely insulated attic room is shown here. Note how the roll insulation is used in the regular fashion on the small knee-wall but crosswise on the other walls because of the unusual spacing of both studs and rafters. It is also good practice to fill in spaces around windows with insulating material as this do-it-yourselfer has done.

To compare two products using different rating systems, you can convert a C or a U number to an R number. Simply divide the number 1 by the C or the U number. If a product has a C or a U number of 0.5, for example, its R number will be 2 (1 ÷ 0.5 = 2). If it has a higher (and therefore less desirable) C or U number such as 2, it will have a lower (and also less desirable) R number (1 ÷ 2 = 0.5).

Always check the ratings when shopping for insulation, and use the numbers to find the best insulation value for your money.

WHERE TO INSULATE

Generally speaking, all outside walls and all ceilings that are exposed to open, raftered areas should be insulated. This applies to garages and to carports or breezeways that you are enclosing. Since the framing in these areas is either new (as in the case of carport walls) or exposed (as in a garage), it is a relatively simple matter to staple blankets, batts, or reflective insulation in place.

If garage walls are already finished off with wallboard or paneling, but are uninsulated, you may be able to pry loose or cut away a section of the wallcovering along the top of the wall and pour loose fill insulation into all openings between studs. If this is not feasible, you are probably better off to call in the professional to blow the insulating material in from outside the walls. If the garage ceiling is finished off, there should be some access via a trapdoor, or perhaps through an attic crawl space from the main part of the house, so that you can pour in loose fill or lay blankets or batts between the ceiling joints.

When you are finishing the attic of a typical story-and-a-half house, the insulation should be run between the floor joists from the eaves to the short knee walls, and then continued up the knee walls between the studs to the rafters. Staple the insulation between the rafters up to the collar beams (now the ceiling joists) and then between the collar beams. The insulation closes off the living area of the finished attic from the unheated crawl spaces at the sides and the area above the ceiling.

Many unfinished attics already have insulation between the floor joists to help keep the heat in the rooms below. If that is the case in your house, you might as well just leave it there rather than go to the trouble of tearing it all out—especially if that would mean ripping up a partial or full subfloor. But you must still place insulation in the new knee wall, between the rafters, and between the ceiling joists.

The thick masonry foundation walls of a basement provide a fair degree of insulation in themselves, along with that of the earth outside the walls. Because of this, further insulation is not normally used on outside walls when finishing off a basement. However, if you live in an area with extremely harsh winters, you may wish the added protection. This will mean furring out the basement walls with thicker lumber than the 1 x 2s or 1 x 3s usually recommended.

If you are finishing off (and heating) only part of the basement and partitioning off the rest for storage or whatever, plan to install insulation in the partition. This will help keep the heat in the living area where it is wanted. You should also insulate between the overhead floor joists in the unheated area to help keep heat in the rooms above. It is not necessary to insulate the ceiling in the heated part of the basement.

Figure 5-4: When insulation is installed, it is usually easier to use the 48″-long friction batts rather than the long blankets. Simply place the batts between joists or rafters. No stapling needed (*courtesy of Owens-Corning Fiberglass*).

Walls & Wallcoverings
6

The do-it-yourselfer faces a pleasant dilemma once the framing of walls and partitions is finished and the insulation is put up: What type of wallcovering should you use? There is an almost endless variety of paneling, usually plywood or hardboard that is often prefinished in wood grains or special effects such as basketweave, flocking, simulated brick, and the like. For walls and ceilings that are to be painted or papered, gypsum wallboard is your most likely choice. (For many types of paneling, it is recommended that gypsum wallboard be installed first as a backing.)

GYPSUM WALLBOARD

Gypsum wallboard is known by many names. Some people call it *drywall*, which refers to the method of application, as opposed to using wet plaster. Others call it *Sheetrock*, which is a brand name of gypsum wallboard produced by United States Gypsum. Still others call it *plasterboard*, which is close to calling it *gypsumboard* (plaster is largely gypsum, a chalky mineral).

By whatever name, gypsum wallboard is gypsum pressed between two sheets of tough paper, and it has been a real boon to the builder and the do-it-yourselfer. Until a decade or so ago, walls were finished by nailing lath to the framing and covering the lath with two or three coats of plaster. Such a wall was very strong and had good insulating qualities, but the method was expensive, difficult, and time-consuming.

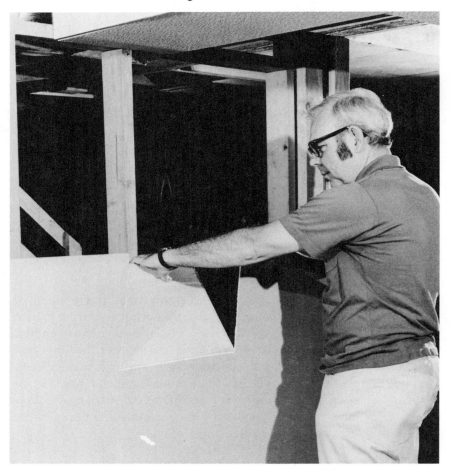

Figure 6-1: A sharp utility knife is used to cut gypsum wallboard panels. Score the face along the cut line, then snap off (*courtesy of Georgia-Pacific*).

With gypsum wallboard, a wall can be covered in a very short time. The wallboard comes in 4 x 8-, 4 x 10-, 4 x 12-, and 4 x 16-foot panels. It can be installed horizontally or vertically, depending on most economical usage. It goes up easily on walls and partitions, although its size and weight make ceiling application difficult for one person—one or two helpers to hold it in place while you nail it will solve that problem.

Figure 6-2: Wallboard panels can be installed horizontally or vertically—and quickly to cover large wall surfaces (*courtesy of Georgia-Pacific*).

Figure 6-3: Annular-ring nails are driven along the edges and into the studs to hold the panels firmly in place (*courtesy of Georgia-Pacific*).

Special annular-ringed nails are recommended for wallboard installation. They should be driven at approximately 4″ intervals around all edges and 6″ intervals into all intermediate studs and joists. Drive the nails slightly into the surface of the wallboard, creating a "dimple."

Nailing is the easy part—finishing requires some practice and patience. *Spackle* (joint compound) is applied to conceal the nailheads, and tape and spackle are applied over the joints between sheets.

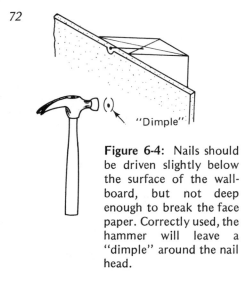

Figure 6-4: Nails should be driven slightly below the surface of the wall-board, but not deep enough to break the face paper. Correctly used, the hammer will leave a "dimple" around the nail head.

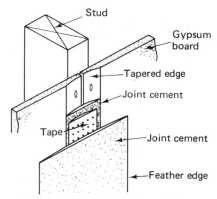

Figure 6-5: Joint treatment between two sheets of gypsum wallboard. Note that edges of the joint compound are feathered into the surface of the wall-board.

Use a wide-blade putty knife to spread the spackle over the nailheads; if the heads show through, drive them below the surface and apply more spackle, smoothing it even with the surface of the wallboard.

Apply a layer of spackle 3″ or so wide along each joint, pressing the knife firmly against the wallboard and drawing it along. Immediately apply the finishing tape, pressing it into the spackle with the knife. Cover the tape with a thin layer of compound.

Inside corners are formed by folding the tape in half and embedding it in spackle as above. For outside corners, a metal beading is used; it is concealed by spackle.

Allow the joint compound on nails and joints to dry overnight. Smooth the spackled areas lightly with sandpaper, and then apply a second coat of spackle. Extend the spackle about 2″ on each side of taped joints, and feather the edges of the spackled areas to meet the surrounding wallboard. Allow these areas to dry for 24 hours.

Apply a final coat of spackle to nailheads and joints, similar to the second coat but feathering the spackle about 2″ beyond the second coat at the joints. Allow to dry. For a final smoothing, use a fine-grade sandpaper wrapped around a sanding block. Do not use a power sander, and be careful not to rough up the face paper of the wallboard. Remove sanding dust from the surface by wiping with a damp cloth. If you've done the job well, nailheads and joints will be invisible. If not, a little more sanding and filling may be in order.

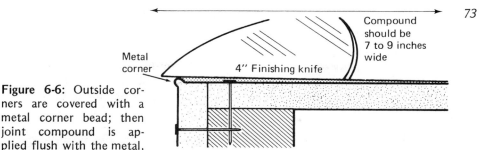

Figure 6-6: Outside corners are covered with a metal corner bead; then joint compound is applied flush with the metal.

Of course, if you are simply putting up the wallboard as a backer for paneling (it adds strength and helps deaden sound), there is no need for spackling and taping. If you are wallpapering over the wallboard, you will still have to spackle and tape, but you don't have to be quite so fussy with your sanding and smoothing, especially if you are using a textured wallpaper. You can also avoid taping joints by covering them with lattice strips or molding. However, you will still have to spackle the nailheads, unless you use the molding at 24" or 16" intervals (which might be a bit much for decor purposes).

WALL PANELING

The most popular types of paneling are tongue-and-grooved natural wood, hardwood veneer plywood, and woodgrain hardboard. Natural wood can be purchased unfinished or prefinished, while hardboard and some veneers come with a plastic coating for wipe-clean maintenance, which is especially desirable where young children will be making extensive use of the room. Unless you are planning a special-effect finish, prefinished paneling should be your choice—when the last panel is in place, the job is done (except, perhaps, for a few moldings).

Paneling may cost anywhere from 10¢ to well over $3 a square foot, according to the type of material and finish, so that will be another factor in your decision. In addition to the familiar wood grains (ranging from "barn siding" to such exotics as pecky cypress), panels may be finished to resemble marble, mosaic, or natural wood flake. Some are embossed to imitate burlap, basketweave, wicker, leather, and other designs. There are even plain panels, in tinted or solid colors, if that is more to your taste.

Most paneling comes in 4x8-foot sheets, although 4x7-foot sheets are also available in some types, while others may come in tongue-and-grooved lumber or 16" wide "planks." If your room is

74   much higher than 8', you may be able to make up the difference
with an extrawide baseboard. Or you can install more paneling to fill
the gap; in that case, leave a painted 1″ horizontal *shadow line*
between the paneling pieces, rather than butting them tightly.
(Molding can go over this later if desired.) Still another possibility is
to install a narrow display shelf at the intersection of the two pieces
of paneling.

Figure 6-7: Natural-wood paneling comes in solid form like the redwood shiplap used here.

Different types of paneling come in different thicknesses, and the thinner ones should be installed over some sort of backing (an existing wall or new gypsumboard) for strength and rigidity. Follow the manufacturer's directions on this.

Figure 6-8: Tongue-and-groove western hemlock has been used to panel this bedroom.

Installation on Studs or Furring

Where no backing is required, the panels are fastened directly to the studs or furring strips. Some types use special clips, but most are simply nailed or glued in place. Gluing is generally recommended for most satisfactory results.

Panels should be allowed to acclimate to the room for at least 48 hours before installation. Separate the panels and stand them on their long edges. During this period, you can install insulation between the furring strips. Staple the insulation to the sides of the strips, leaving the faces clear for panel adhesive.

76 You can cut paneling with a crosscut hand saw (rather difficult), a table saw (face up), or a portable or saber saw (face down). Allow about one inch for clearance in cutting panels to height; this will be concealed by molding later on.

Figure 6-9: Hardwood plywood consists of a thin layer of handsome, expensive natural wood bonded to several layers of a lower grade wood. This way, you pay a premium only for the visi- ble surface. Weldwood hickory paneling is used at the left and Georgia-Pacific's Old World veneer at the right. The latter comes in pecan, oak, cedar and birch.

Start at one corner of the room, and use a caulking gun to apply a bed of panel adhesive on the full face of each stud or furring strip to be covered by the first panel. Set the panel in place with small wedges beneath. Use a carpenter's level to make sure that the outside edge of the panel is perfectly plumb—if it isn't, you'll have trouble with each succeeding panel in the room. If you have to pull the panel slightly away from the corner at the top or bottom to plumb it, don't worry; that will be covered later by the adjacent panel or by corner molding. Make sure that the outer edge of the panel falls over the middle of a stud or furring strip. If it doesn't, take down the panel and trim it at the *corner* edge.

When you are satisfied with the positioning of the panel, drive a few nails along the top edge to hold it in place (these, too, will be hidden with molding). Then pull the panel away from the wall, and block it out at the bottom with a piece of scrap wood—the nails at the top will keep it from sliding out of position. Allow the

Figure 6-10: Permaneer Brazilian Rosewood is a woodgrain hardboard which makes an attractive paneled wall.

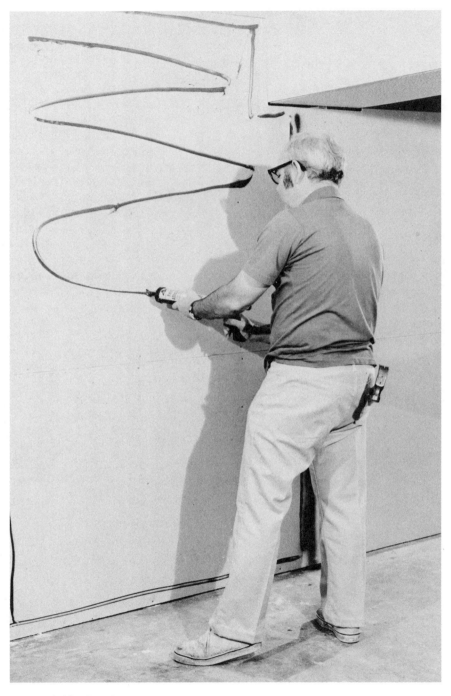

Figure 6-11: Paneling adhesive is applied to the backerboard in a squiggly pattern (*courtesy of Georgia-Pacific*).

adhesive to dry for about 10 minutes, and then make a squiggly pattern (see Figure 6-11) or a large "**X**" in the middle. Set the panel in place, and proceed as above—plumbing, nailing at the top, and pulling the panel away to let the adhesive dry before pressing the panel firmly in place. Continue as above until all panels are installed.

Figure 6-12: Among the many hardboard panels available are these two used effectively for two quite different decorating themes. At the left the room wall is finished with Masonite Ceylon teak while the dining room at the right is paneled with Casa Blanca simulated stucco.

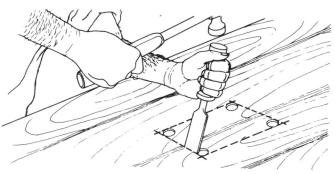

Figure 6-13: To make a "pocket cut" for electrical outlets, drill holes at four corners and cut between them with a chisel or keyhole saw (*courtesy of Bruce-Ply Paneling*).

Here's a tip from the professionals that will be especially appreciated by the do-it-yourselfer. Before putting up each panel, spray a line of black paint on the backerboard where the panel edges will fall. In the highly unlikely event that your panel joints are slightly less than perfect, the black paint will camouflage the backerboard which otherwise would be highly visible—just in case . . . .

Figure 6-14: Press each panel against the adhesive, then out from the gypsum board for a few minutes to let the adhesive set. (Wedge a block of wood behind the panel if you don't want to hold it that long.) When the adhesive is nearly dry, press the panel against the backerboard and fasten it with a few finishing nails.

Figure 6-15: Spray a matching paint on the board where the panel grooves will meet. This background color masks any nicks in paneling edges or slight misalignments (*courtesy of Georgia-Pacific*).

Figure 6-16: Paneling—in this case Georgia-Pacific's Silverado—is tacked at the top while the adhesive sets.

Moldings

Matching moldings are available for most prefinished paneling; some even include nails with heads colored to match, so all you need do is drive them flush with the surface. If you use regular finishing nails, they should be set below the surface of the molding and the holes filled with matching wood putty.

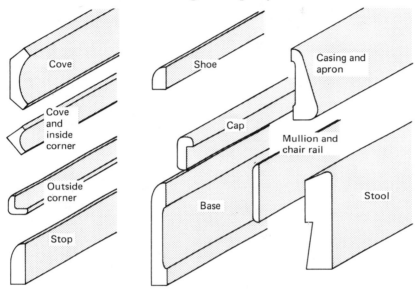

Figure 6-17: Many paneling manufacturers make matching moldings that are designed for each type of paneling—like this Bruce-Ply.

Moldings are installed at the ceiling line and baseboard (but only after the ceiling and floor have been installed). Where the moldings meet at corners, you can either *miter* them (cut them both at 45-degree angles like a picture frame) or *cope* them (cut one molding to fit the curve of the other). This decision will depend on the type of molding you choose.

Since moldings give your job a really professional look, you should try to cut and position them as accurately as humanly possible. A wooden miter box is one step forward, but better yet is a metal miter box, adjustable for every point on the compass. With your box, you should also have a good backsaw, a squarish-looking tool with a reinforcing band along the back of the blade to keep it straight and to give it a little extra weight.

Properly used, the backsaw and miter box should give you cuts so accurate that two 45-degree cuts should meet in a perfect

82 right angle with no "air" between. If you think this is easy without the proper tools, try it. You can even goof it up *with* the right tools.

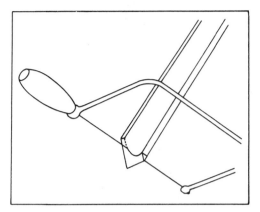 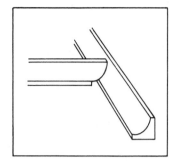

Figure 6-18: How to use a coping saw properly to cope moldings.

Quarter-round moldings, casings, lattice stock, and other straight moldings lend themselves easily to miter cuts, but ceiling and other "fancy" moldings generally do not work very well when cut at 45 degrees. To *cope* such a molding, set it upright in the miter box in the same position it will be on the wall. Hold it against the backplate, and trim it at a 45-degree angle. The remaining profile serves as a guideline for the coping saw, which is used to trim away the wedge at another 45-degree angle. In other words, saw away the excess along the mitered line so that the angle from front to back of the molding is again 90 degrees (see Figure 6-18). The resultant curve should fit nicely against the face of the adjoining molding.

Here are a few more molding tips:

* In general, outside corners should be mitered. Inside corners are usually coped, depending on the type of molding (ask your supplier).
* For a tight miter joint, nail and glue at each joint.
* Where wall irregularities occur, nail at the gaps to pull the molding tight against the wall.
* Drive nails into the grooves of patterned moldings.
* Where fancy moldings intersect, at least one should be symmetrical. If neither pattern is symmetrical, a *butt block* or a square, flat piece of wood should be inserted at the intersection, and the moldings butted against that.
* To cover a long stretch that requires more than one piece of molding, the joint should be *scarfed* (cut at matching angles) instead of installed with a 90-degree butt.

Moldings come in many shapes and sizes, and are a godsend   *83*
to the do-it-yourselfer who has gone a little awry in cutting
the panels. If you cut a perfect inside corner with your paneling, you
may not need molding, but outside corners should have molding
anyway because of the rough treatment a corner gets. Whenever you
have a problem getting a perfect fit, there is a molding of some sort
to bail you out.

There are some plastic moldings for panel and ceiling joints
that hardly show at all. Usually, these must be applied before the
panel is installed, and the panel then slides into the molding. When
you pick out your paneling, select the molding along with it. Your
building supply dealer will guide you if you have any questions.

GETTING THE HANG OF WALLPAPER

Almost all wallpapers today are pretrimmed, which saves an
enormous amount of time as well as most of the frustration. The
one notable exception is flocked paper, much of which comes untrimmed. Untrimmed papers are an extra burden for the amateur and
should not be tried until you've mastered the basic papering skills.

Most manufacturers will include directions with their papers,
and these should always be followed. Pay particular attention to the
type of adhesive recommended by the manufacturer or dealer. Vinyl
papers, for example, need a type of adhesive different from that used
for conventional papers.

There are several ways to determine the number of single
rolls you need. First and most important, you must know the
dimensions of the walls to be covered. A simple room-estimating
chart appears in almost every sample book (and on p. 85). If you are
confused, just ask the dealer, who will be glad to figure the number
of rolls for you. Should you wish to figure the number of rolls the
way the experts do, use the following method.

Example: A living room is 10′ wide and 15′ long with a 9′
ceiling, two doors, and one window.

First, you measure how many *running feet* of wall space you
wish to decorate and then multiply that total by the height of the
room or of the wall to be decorated. In this example, 10′ plus 15′
plus 10′ plus 15′ equals 50′ feet (circumference of the room); 50′
multiplied by 9′ (height of room) equals 450 square feet (total wall
space).

Every single roll of wallcovering covers about 30 square feet.
Wallcoverings are priced by the single roll and packaged in two-roll or

84   three-roll bolts to reduce waste and to give you more full-length strips. A single roll gives you 2-1/2 normal strips, and a double roll, 5. To find the number of single rolls you need, divide the total square footage of wall space by 30 square feet. Dividing 450 square feet by 30 square feet gives you 15 single rolls. (See Table 6-1 for exact amounts.)

Generally, the final step is to count the number of doors or windows in the room, and deduct one roll of wallcovering for every two windows or doors. In the example given, there are two doors and one window, so you deduct one roll for a total of 14 rolls. (If there were one more window, you would deduct another roll for a total of 13 single rolls.)

It is always advisable to overestimate your needs slightly. You should have a little paper in reserve for repairs in the event some area becomes damaged. It is difficult to get a perfect match in color shading, should you have to reorder from a different printing run to make up for underestimating. Keep track of the run number; it is as important as the batch number is for paint. Better yet, have an extra roll stashed away somewhere.

Now that you know how many rolls you need, you can look confidently for the perfect pattern. It is important to remember when selecting patterns that they have actually been tested on walls. What might appear to be too bold a pattern in the sample book actually will add distinctive character to a room without being overpowering.

Simple Tools & Equipment—A Good Beginning

The few simple tools you will need are a plumb line, chalk, a stepladder or stool, a yardstick, scissors, a sponge, a seam roller, a single-edge razor blade or razor blade knife, a wide-bladed putty knife or straightedge, and a flat surface, such as the kitchen table, to work on. Many retailers rent paperhanging tables and tools for very small fees. If you have unpasted wallcoverings, you will also need a paste brush or paint roller and a bucket.

Before you begin hanging a pattern, prepare your walls by removing any loose old wallpaper and all electrical switch and outlet plates. When there are more than two or three layers of paper already on the wall, all the old paper should be steamed off. Your wallcovering dealer should be able to rent you a machine for this. Fill all cracks and holes in the walls with spackling compound; then sand the patched areas smooth and glue-size. (All unpainted plaster, gypsum wallboard, and hardboard should be glue-sized.)

Start at the right of the door leading into the room and measure to a point 1 inch less than the width of the wallcovering. Tack a weighted chalked string at this point and let it hang freely. Holding the string taut at the baseboard, snap the string against the wall. The vertical chalk line is your starting point.

The right-hand side of your first strip should be positioned along this line. The left-hand side of the next strip also will be on this line and butted against, not overlapping, the right-hand side of the first strip. All new wallcoverings, other than hand-prints, are electrically pre-trimmed for perfect seamless matching.

Unroll your wallcovering, pattern side up, and pull it gently but firmly over the edge of the table to remove curl. Measure and cut your first strip with scissors, making sure you have an extra three or four inches at the top and the bottom for matching and trimming. On very large patterns, you may need even more than this for your following strips, so always check where your match will be before cutting the next strip. Professionals often cut more than one strip at a time, but for those who don't hang wallcoverings that often, one strip at a time is safer. It is wise, however, to cut the next strip

Table 6-1: WALLCOVERING ESTIMATING CHART FOR WALLPAPER

*Distance Around Room in Feet	Single Rolls for Wall Areas by Ceiling Heights:			Number of yards for Borders	Single Rolls for Ceilings	*Distance Around Room in Feet	Single Rolls for Wall Areas by Ceiling Heights:			Number of yards for Borders	Single Rolls for Ceilings
	8 feet	9 feet	10 feet				8 feet	9 feet	10 feet		
28	8	8	10	11	2	60	14	16	18	21	8
30	8	8	10	11	2	62	14	16	20	22	8
32	8	8	10	12	2	64	16	18	20	23	8
34	8	10	10	13	4	66	16	18	20	23	10
36	8	10	10	13	4	68	16	18	20	24	10
38	10	10	12	14	4	70	16	20	20	25	10
40	10	10	12	15	4	72	18	20	20	25	12
42	10	12	12	15	4	74	18	20	22	26	12
44	10	12	14	16	4	76	18	20	22	27	12
46	12	12	14	17	6	78	18	20	22	27	14
48	12	12	14	17	6	80	20	20	24	28	14
50	12	14	14	18	6	82	20	22	24	29	14
52	12	14	16	19	6	84	20	22	24	30	16
54	14	14	16	19	6	86	20	22	24	30	16
56	14	14	16	20	8	88	20	22	26	31	16
58	14	16	18	21	8	90	20	24	26	32	18

*Deduct one single roll for every two ordinary size doors or windows or every 30 square feet of opening.

before hanging the previous one. Remember, you don't have to finish the job in one evening—you can always do a few strips at a time. Unlike paint, nothing will show where you stopped and started again.

Pre-Pasted Paper

Place the water box against the baseboard where you are working; then half fill it with warm water. (Water boxes are available free or for a nominal charge from your dealer.) Don't try filling the box and carrying it to the spot. You're bound to spill some on the way. Place a newspaper underneath the box before filling it; then you can easily slide the water box on the paper to the spot where you will hang each new strip. Put the ladder in position to hang the wallcovering after the water box is positioned.

Taking your pre-cut strip, roll it up loosely, paste side out; then submerge the roll completely in the water box for as long as recommended by the manufacturer (usually 30 seconds). Holding the top of the strip, slowly unroll the wallcovering from the water box, stepping up the ladder at the same time. Make certain that all of the paste is wet.

Press the top of the wallcovering against the wall, allowing a few inches to overlap onto the ceiling. Keeping the right edge against the chalk line, smooth the wallcovering against the wall with a clean, damp sponge or cloth, removing all wrinkles and air bubbles. Gently press the wallcovering into the corner with your fingers. Then, using the wide-bladed putty knife or straightedge as a guide between the razor blade and the wall, cut off the excess at the ceiling and baseboard.

Slide the water box to the spot where the next strip will be hung and repeat the same procedure, matching the pattern and butting the left edge of the second strip with the right edge of the first. Do *not* overlap. Wipe off all excess adhesive from the ceiling, baseboards, moldings, and wallcovering with a damp sponge or cloth before the paste dries.

Unpasted Paper

Mix the paste according to the manufacturer's instructions. Place the wallcovering, pattern side down, on your table, and apply a thin coat of paste to the top third of the strip. Fold this third over onto itself, paste to paste, to keep it from drying while you paste the remaining two-thirds. When finished pasting, fold the bottom two-thirds onto itself in the same way. Do not crease these folds. Carry the strip to the plumbed area, unfold the top third, and press it to the wall, allowing a few inches to extend onto the ceiling. Then smooth the wallcovering with a damp cellulose or natural sponge or with a paperhanger's brush.

Figure 6-19: Brush paste on one-third of the wallpaper strip first; then fold it onto itself, paste-side to paste-side. Next, paste the bottom two-thirds and fold it onto itself. If you use a pre-pasted paper, you will dip it into a waterbox instead (*courtesy of The Birge Company*).

Unfold the bottom two-thirds, and, keeping the right edge aligned with the chalk line, smooth out all wrinkles and air bubbles. Remove the excess paper at the ceiling and baseboard by gently pressing the wallcovering into the corner with your fingers and using the wide-bladed putty knife or straightedge as a guide for trimming

88 with the razor blade. Wipe off all excess adhesive from the ceiling, baseboards, moldings, and wallcovering with a damp sponge or cloth before the paste dries.

Though the same basic methods are used for applying flocks as for other wallcoverings, extra care is required in some instances. Note whether your flock wallcovering is made of acrylic or rayon flocking. Acrylic flocks are stain-proof and crush-resistant, while rayon flocks are not. Be sure to follow the manufacturer's instructions in applying flocks. Acrylic flocks, either pre-pasted or unpasted, can usually be applied the same way as other papers.

Figure 6-20: The first piece of wallpaper is butted against plumb chalkline; then second piece is butted (**not** overlapped) against the first one. **Note** how bottom of strip is kept folded until top has been matched, then it is smoothed down with brush or sponge.

Figure 6-21: Next, a seam roller is run down the edges. Then the end strip is carried around the corner and smoothed down. About one inch is cut off on the right, back from the corner. Then a plumb line is run again in the corner and a new strip is started.

Ceilings, Corners, etc.

Ceiling strips should be hung across the shorter dimensions of the room. It is best to work standing on a sturdy plank supported by two stepladders. Ceilings are easier to handle when two persons are working, with one holding part of the strip while the other places and smooths the rest of the strip on the ceiling. The same procedures are used for ceilings that are used for walls, except that strips are accordion folded, paste side to paste side, for ease of handling. Start in the most visible area and finish in the least visible, ending over the entrance to the room, for example.

On both inside and outside corners, your walls may not be perfectly straight, so you should always cut the wallcovering to extend around the corner about an inch. Then snap another plumb line to make sure that the right-hand side of the strip is vertical. This portion should overlap the 1-inch extension around the corner (the only time overlapping is allowed). The extension around the corner should be feather-edged by sanding, and if it is a flocked pattern, all flocking on the extension should be removed.

The slanting walls of a dormer or refinished attic are subject to the same rules: Carry all strips around corners and angles about 1 inch. Mismatches are bound to happen, so a pattern with an informal scattering of flowers or other items will disguise these areas best. Light, open patterns will help to "raise" sloping walls visually. So it is best to carry patterns up the wall to normal ceiling level rather than stopping at the start of the sloping areas.

When working around electrical outlets and switches, smooth the strip down to the outlet or just below it. Press the paper gently and mark the area; then cut out around the noticeable outline. Proceed with caution while cutting wet wallcoverings around live electrical outlets. Mark the area to be cut; then pull strip away from wall to snip out hole. This will avoid electrical shock. If you would like to disguise your outlet and switch covers, they can be covered easily with some of the left-over wallcovering scraps to add a look of craftsmanship to your work.

If possible, remove or loosen all wall fixtures so you can work beneath them. A slit can be cut into the wallcovering to work it around a fixture; then press it back together for an invisible seam when the wallcovering is smoothed down.

Don't try to pre-cut wallcoverings to go around obstructions. Match up the edge of each new strip with the previous one, and smooth it down as far as possible; then begin your trimming. To go around a window or door, cut at a 45-degree angle into the corner so you can use your straightedge and razor blade to do the trim cutting against the side of the window or door. Trim along all moldings or extensions from a wall just as you do along the baseboard.

You can work around pipes under sinks and elsewhere by slitting the wallcovering from the nearest side; then press the wallcovering around the pipe and trim it to fit. The slit will make an

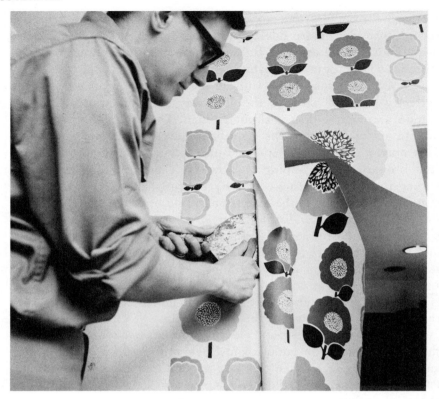

Figure 6-22: Cutting around doors and windows is easier if you first press the wallpaper into the corner with a straightedge, then cut into the corner with a razor blade knife held at a 45-degree angle.

invisible seam when the wallcovering is smoothed against the wall. Many pipes have a piece of metal trim to hide the hole in the wall. This trim slides easily from the wall while you work and, when replaced, covers the edge of the wallcovering around the pipe.

Allow the pasted wallcovering to hang down behind the radiator after you have smoothed the upper portion to the wall completely. Using a long-handled, clean paint roller or yardstick, lightly smooth out the paper behind the radiator so it is reasonably well pressed against the wall. It is best to wrap the yardstick with a piece of cloth to avoid damaging the wallcovering. The alternative is to remove the radiator while applying the wallcovering, but this is a lot of work and usually unnecessary.

You can brighten up an old door with wallcovering in the panels or add new life to plain kitchen cabinets by covering them with a cheerful pattern. There are hundreds of other places you can use wallcoverings, too. Cover phones, dressers, tables, window shades, and lamp shades; or cut out the figures in a pattern and paste them on chairs, lamps, wastebaskets, an infant's crib—anywhere you want to add a little extra touch of color.

Figure 6-23: Start on the ceiling when painting a room. Use a brush to "cut in" the corners and edges, and adapt the plank-and-ladder technique for safe, fast work (*courtesy of Benjamin Moore & Company*).

INTERIOR PAINTING

Just as today's wallcoverings have been improved to make doing it yourself easier, so have modern paints been updated, making application simpler. The *only* paint for most interior uses is latex. It goes on easily and dries quickly, with excellent covering qualities. More important for the do-it-yourselfer, however, is the fact that cleanup chores are drastically curtailed because latex is almost dripless and is water-soluble. No need to soak the brush in mineral spirits and thinners—a little bit of water, and both you and your brushes are set for another day.

Latex paints now come in semi-gloss and enamels for both interior and exterior applications, so it is possible to paint your entire home with latex. There are, however, occasions when other paints will do a better or more durable job. Table 6-2 will help guide you to the proper selection. In most cases though, you can't go wrong using latex.

New Techniques for New Paints

The newer products now on the market differ from conventional paints not only in performance but also in application technique. It is particularly important to read the instructions on the label carefully. Unless you follow the advice of the manufacturer, you may not get the desired result. The newer paints will not work out very well, in many cases, if you handle them as you would the old-fashioned paints.

Certain *catalyzed* coatings, for example, must be applied to a meticulously cleaned surface. If you do not have time to prepare the surface as required, you'll do better to use a conventional type of paint. Too many people tend to brush out or roll out paint, but the new, paste-like coatings are not intended to be thinned, and will not give full satisfaction if spread too thin.

On any painting project, remember two things: Use paints that are clearly labeled for interior application, and allow time for proper surface preparation—cleansing, patching, and smoothing. Painted walls require the same type of preparation as papered walls, but the finish must be even smoother, since paint will not hide the imperfections like paper does.

Painting Ceilings

Ceilings are important light-reflecting surfaces in most rooms and should have dull-surfaced coatings that reflect light evenly. In bathrooms and kitchens, however, semi-gloss or enamel finishes are generally more desirable because of their washability. Plaster and wallboard ceilings can be coated with a flat oil-base paint or with semi-gloss, emulsion, or rubber-base paints, as well as casein and latex. If the ceiling has not been previously painted, a primer should be applied before using enamel or semi-gloss paint. On acoustic tile, use flat paint, thinned in accordance with your dealer's recommendations (but don't paint tile at all unless you have to).

Table 6-2: WHAT TO USE INSIDE A ROOM—AND WHERE

FINISHES* FOR INTERIOR SURFACES

Interior surface	Flat enamel	Semi-gloss enamel	Gloss enamel	Interior varnish	Shellac-Lacquer	Wax (liquid or paste)	Wax (emulsion)	Stain	Wood sealer	Floor varnish	Floor paint or enamel	Aluminum paint	Undercoater or Sealer	Metal primer	Latex flat (wall)	Latex gloss & semi-gloss
MASONRY:																
Asphalt tile					Xp	Xp	X									
Concrete floors							Xp	X			X					
Bathroom & Kitchen walls		Xp	Xp												X	Xp
Linoleum						X	X									
New masonry	Xp	Xp											X		X	Xp
Old masonry	X	X										X	X		X	Xp
Plaster walls & Ceiling	Xp	Xp											X		X	Xp
Vinyl & Rubber tile floors					X	X	X									
Wallboard	Xp	Xp											X		X	Xp
METAL:																
Aluminum windows	Xp	Xp		X								X	X	X	Xp	Xp
Heating ducts	Xp	Xp		X								X	X	X	Xp	Xp
Heating pipes & Radiators	Xp	Xp		X								X	X		Xp	Xp
Steel cabinets	Xp	Xp		X	X									X	Xp	Xp
Steel windows	Xp	Xp		X	X							X		X		Xp
WOOD:																
Floors	Xp						Xp	Xp	X	Xp	Xp					Xp
Paneling	Xp	Xp						X							Xp	Xp
Stair risers				X				X	X							
Stair treads				X				X	X	X	X					
Trim	Xp	Xp			X								X		Xp	Xp
Window sills	Xp														Xp	Xp

*Xp indicates that a primer or sealer may be necessary before the finishing coat—unless the surface has been previously finished.

Figure 6-24: Use a paint roller for good, quick coverage of wide surfaces (*courtesy of Benjamin Moore & Company*).

Interior Walls

Latex paints are often described by the chemical from which the latex emulsion is made—synthetic rubber, vinyl, or acrylic. You will find latex paint easy to apply by brush or roller. Most people find it easiest to "cut in" the edges and corners first with a brush and then use a roller in a "W" pattern.

Alkyd paints have come into use in relatively recent years as the result of chemical modification of linseed oil. Alkyd-painted walls are more washable than most and have excellent hiding power (they keep underneath color from showing through). One coat of alkyd paint will sometimes suffice where two coats of latex may be needed.

Where a flat oil paint is to be used, it should be preceded by a sealer. Most flat oil-base paints, incidentally, are not recommended for kitchen or bathroom walls. Here, enamel or semi-gloss latex, a rubber-base, or a suitable emulsion paint will give more satisfactory service. For rooms other than the kitchen or bathroom, emulsion, rubber-base, and casein paints—in addition to flat oil paint—can be used. On newly plastered walls, where adequate drying time cannot be allowed before painting is begun, it is important to apply a lime-resistant or alkali-resistant paint that will not be affected by the chemical action of wet lime.

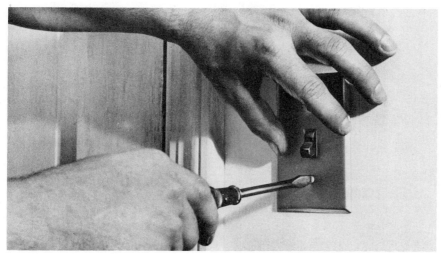

Figure 6-25: Painting will be a lot easier if you prepare for it by removing switch plates and other obstacles.

Interior Trim

In most cases, the same paint—and the same color—that is used on the walls can be applied to the wood or metal trim. Utilizing the same color on walls and trim is especially advisable in smaller rooms to avoid a cluttered appearance. Where there are likely to be wear and finger marks, such as on doors, door frames, and window sills, apply a semi-gloss enamel matching the color of the wall paint. It's a good practice to give wood an enamel undercoat, followed by any suitable top coat, for greater durability and hiding power.

On woodwork that is new and that is to have an opaque coating, use semi-gloss, enamel, or flat paint. Either oil or latex is suitable. Keep in mind, however, that flat paint is easily soiled and thus is an inferior choice for window sills. Emulsion and rubber-base paints are also acceptable for woodwork. All of these coatings can also be used on woods that have been previously painted or

96 varnished. Before painting over such surfaces, make sure that all traces of wax have been removed and that any still-glossy surface has been sanded so that the new coating can adhere firmly.

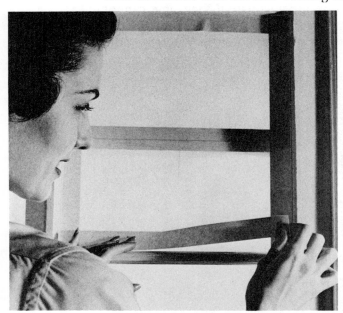

Figure 6-26: Put masking tape on the window panes and similar surfaces that are not to be painted—before you begin, of course.

Figure 6-27: Teamwork makes painting simpler for everyone. One person works ahead "cutting in," while the other follows, doing the wider surfaces with a roller.

Where there is to be a radical change of color, more than one coat of paint may be required; if enamel or semi-gloss is to be used, an enamel undercoat should be applied first. Follow the manufacturer's directions on this.

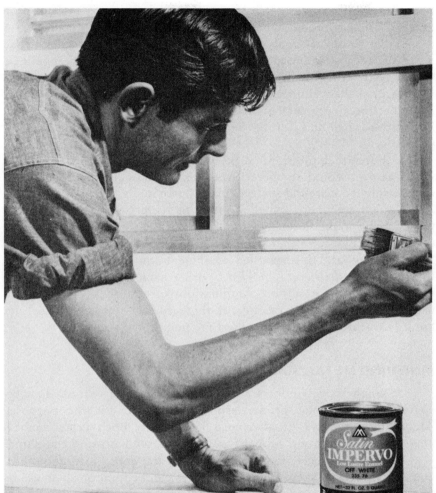

Figure 6-28: Use semi-gloss enamels for woodwork, but apply an enamel undercoat or flat paint first.

UNFINISHED PANELING

Most paneling today comes pre-finished, so that you need only glue or nail it to the wall, install moldings, and enjoy. This is true not only for pre-finished hardboards or plastic finishes but also for hardwood-veneer paneling.

There are, however, unfinished panelings that are less expensive for those who have the inclination to do their own finishing. Some woods, such as redwood and western red cedar, come unfinished and don't need any finishing, although for interior use, you may want to give them a coat of sealer, varnish, or shellac. (For exterior use, both redwood and red cedar are best left unfinished.)

To finish materials like pine, Philippine mahogany, etc., that are not factory-finished, first apply a wood filler to open-grained woods. After this, the wood may be stained if desired, followed by varnish or shellac, and then several thin coats of good paste wax, well buffed. (For a complete discussion of wood finishing, see our book *Furniture Repair and Refinishing* published by the Reston Publishing Company in 1974.)

For either pre-finished or self-finished paneling, care for the wood as you would any fine furniture. Use wax or furniture polish occasionally to keep the surface looking rich and glowing.

You *can* paint paneling, but this seems self-defeating unless the paneling looks seriously outdated, marked up, or ugly. When so doing, paint like any other woodwork, as described above.

There are finishes that combine both clear and pigmented finishes called *driftwood*, *pickled* or other names. These are specialty finishes and call for certain combinations of materials. Consult your paint dealer for advice on any of these special finishes, or see our book *Furniture Repair and Refinishing* mentioned above.

FINISHING METAL SURFACES

When steel windows are to be painted, they should first be coated with a metal primer especially devised for the purpose. Aluminum windows usually need no primer. Both types can be coated with aluminum, rubber-base, enamel, semi-gloss, or flat paint.

Heating ducts, radiators, and heating pipes also require a metal primer. The same types of coatings can be used on them as are suitable for steel windows. Steel cabinets call for a metal primer, too. Over the primer, you can use a rubber-base, enamel, flat, or semi-gloss latex.

NOVELTY EFFECTS

You can add distinction to a room, and have fun doing it, by introducing novelty touches in paint texture or color. Several of the more recent latex and alkyd products are *thixotropic*, which means

Figure 6-29: HOW TO PAINT WINDOWS AND DOORS

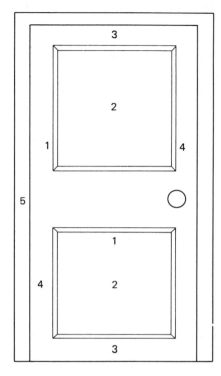

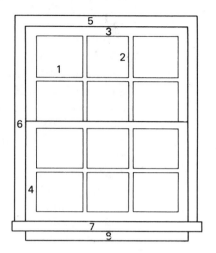

Open each window. First paint the horizontal (**1**) and vertical (**2**) strips or mullions between panes. Next do the frame around upper sash (**3**), then lower sash (**4**). Then paint the top of casing (**5**) and sides (**6**). Finally, paint the sill (**7**), and last, the apron (**8**).

Start by painting the door molding between panels and the frame (1), working from top down. Next paint the panels (2), then the horizontal framing (3). Next paint the vertical framing or stiles (4). Now open the door and paint the casing (5). And finally, paint the door jamb.

that they have a thick, almost jelly-like consistency (which accounts for one of their greatest advantages—driplessness).

By using a wire brush or a sponge after applying a heavy layer of such paint, you can create swirls, stipples, and similar texture effects. Or, for one wall, you might decide to use a multi-color paint, available in spray cans, for an unusual design. At one time you could buy rollers with a built-in design so that you could add a decorative border around the ceiling or create an entire wall pattern. Some of the most popular effects were mottled, stucco-like, or "sand" coats. These rather ingenious devices seem to have disappeared, however.

DECORATING TIPS: As discussed earlier, you should have a certain theme in mind for your rooms long before you put up the framing. Paneling is generally limited to wood tones, but paper and

100   paint are available in an almost infinite variety, so some basic color knowledge is essential. Study a color wheel or, better still, consult any basic art book.

Here are a few decorating tips:

* *Think of the effect* When picking colors, consider the overall impression you wish to make. Red, for example, is an exciting hue, but overwhelming in large doses. It also tends to make a room look smaller. Yellow is cheerful, like sunlight, and its lighter tints provide a sense of spaciousness. Green is tranquil, like a well-groomed lawn. Blue is soothing.

* *Putting color to work* To shorten a long room, use a warm color such as yellow or yellow-orange—or a deep shade of a cool color like green—on the end walls. Use light colors to increase dimensions of a small room. Visually eliminate architectural defects like radiators or old-fashioned molding (unless, of course, your effect *is* old-fashioned) by making them the same color as the surrounding area. To accent a desirable feature, like a fireplace, paint it (if at all) to contrast with the walls.

* *Effect of line* Use horizontal lines to diminish the effect of high ceilings, and vertical lines for low ceilings. Patterns must correspond with the size of the rooms. Don't use too large a pattern in a small room.

* *Warm and cool* Warm colors range from yellow to red. They are stimulating, bright, and spirited. Cool colors are mainly the blues and greens. They are quiet, restful, and soothing. Each room should contain a mixture of warm and cool colors, with warm colors emphasized in a windowless room.

* *Proportion* Proper proportion consists of *not* giving colors "equal time." One color in each room should always be dominant. In large areas, use lighter shades. Vivid colors should be used sparingly.

* *Experiment* Most rooms are dull because of too little imagination. Experiment and be bold, but use neutral colors when being brave.

Floors and Ceilings

7

For some reason, floors and ceilings are often lumped together when we think about or plan home improvements. That really doesn't make much sense when you consider how far apart they really are. Not just bottom and top, but rather in terms of function and of materials available for each.

Flooring materials take more punishment than any other product in your house. They are constantly stomped and scuffed; in nasty weather they must cope with wet boots and shoes, while during the hot days of summer they will often be abraded by dusty and sandy feet. The wonder is that they bear up nearly as well as they do.

Ceilings, on the other hand, need not be nearly as durable. Their function is primarily just to be there. You are far more likely to notice the absence of a ceiling (in a basement, for example) than its presence.

There may be some paradox in the fact that there is a far greater choice of flooring materials (which should be primarily utilitarian) than ceiling materials (primarily decorative). But rather than ponder that philosophical point, rejoice in the selection that you are offered. Underfoot, the do-it-yourselfer can choose from a wide range of resilient flooring and carpeting, both available in tile and roll form, plus hardwood flooring, which also comes in "tiles" or blocks as well as the more conventional tongue-and-groove strips.

102   You can even, in certain situations, opt for painting the floor. Overhead, you will generally choose between tiles and a suspended panel system, or install conventional drywall (see Chapter 6).

FINISHING THE FLOOR

Preparing the Floor

Floor preparation depends on the materials you will use for finishing, as well as what is already there. In the attic, you may have to begin with a subfloor, generally of C-D grade plywood or 6″ tongue-and-groove boards laid at right angles to or diagonally across the joists. Looks are not important here, but the surface should be smooth and free of loose knots.

All flooring materials should be laid over a level surface free of cracks, holes, or other defects. Methods of accomplishing this vary, and it is best to follow instructions given by the manufacturer of the finish flooring. Most wood flooring, resilient tiles, and roll flooring can be laid directly over plywood or hardboard underlayment. The hardboard should be installed with staggered joints, and nailed or stapled at 4″ intervals around the edges and at 6″ intervals over the entire surface. You can rent a special nailing tool that will speed this work considerably. Allow the thickness of a dime (approximately one thirty-seconds of an inch) between panels to permit expansion.

Figure 7-1: An automatic nailer speeds the installation of hardboard underlayment which is laid "rough" side up.

Figure 7-2: Resilient tile is one of the many varieties of flooring material available to the quality conscious do-it-yourselfer.

Figure 7-3: Many types of floor tile are available. This is Armstrong's Solarian Place'n Press in a random chip pattern.

If the finish flooring is to be applied directly to concrete, it is essential to prepare the surface properly. First, remove all loose particles and dust with a wire brush. Fill cracks and small holes with crack filler or concrete patch. Larger damaged areas should be resurfaced and troweled smooth. Uneven and rough areas require leveling, as do expansion joints, if tile or carpeting is to be installed.

Use a very thin asphalt cement that is alkali- and moisture-resistant as a primer to seal porous and dusty concrete.

Make sure that the floor is firm and free of moisture, dust, solvent, scaling paint, wax, oil, grease, asphalt, sealing compound, and all other extraneous materials. Use an alkali-type cleaner or a solution of trisodium phosphate to remove surface oil and grease. Rinse the floor with water, and allow it to dry thoroughly before applying the finishing material. Allow new concrete surfaces to age at least 60 days before painting or tiling.

Floor Paints

The quickest and easiest concrete floor covering to use is paint, either a latex or an epoxy concrete enamel. Unpainted concrete should first be *scarified* (roughened) with etching acid, applied with a plastic sprinkling can. Flush and rinse the floor thoroughly with plenty of clean water to remove all acid, traces of dirt, and surface residue from the pores; sweep the floor vigorously while rinsing. Let it dry for two days before painting.

Latex paint is easily applied with a long-handled roller and a brush for getting into corners. Two coats are recommended. Epoxy enamel must first be mixed in a bucket or other suitable container. It is then applied with brush and long-handled roller. After overnight drying, apply a second coat.

Floor Tiles

There is a tremendous selection of colors and patterns available in floor tiles, so you should have no trouble finding something to your liking. If you wish to customize your floor, just use your imagination. Instead of all one style or pattern in one or two colors, how about using three or even four colors? Or a striped or zigzag pattern in two or more contrasting or complementary colors? Or perhaps you want to separate the room into various functional zones with different tile patterns or different shadings of the same pattern. Still another possibility is to border the entire room with tiles of a color contrasting with the main floor.

Special tile inserts are also available. For the family room, a shuffleboard pattern is popular, but your room should be at least 25' long for a shuffleboard court. Inserts of yachting flags, cocktail glasses, and sports symbols such as bowling pins, tennis rackets, golf clubs, and baseball bats are also popular. Many homeowners use monogram initial inserts to help personalize the room.

Figure 7-4: Azrock's "Montclair" is a vinyl asbestos tile that makes an attractive floor covering for a room with traditional furnishings.

Whatever special effect you decide to use—and the possibilities are limitless—work it out carefully on paper beforehand. Follow your plan carefully during installation to avoid errors that will be difficult or impossible to correct after the job is finished.

Figure 7-5: Kingston (*left*) and Palacio del Sol (*right*) are also floor tiles made by Azrock.

Floor tiles come in various sizes. If the ones you select are the 12 x 12-inch variety, it's simple to figure your needs—the number of tiles will be the same as the square footage of the room, plus a few spares to allow for cutting around the edges and possible damage during installation. Similarly, if the tiles measure 12 x 24-inches, you will need half as many tiles as the room's square footage, plus a few extra. But if the tiles are the more common 9 x 9-inch variety, it takes a bit more math. A 9 x 9 tile is 9/16 of a square foot; so there are 16 9 x 9 tiles to each square yard. A 12 x 15-foot floor, 20 square yards, would require 320 9 x 9-inch tiles, plus spares. Another way to figure need is to measure the length and width of the room, convert these to inches, divide each dimension by nine, and multiply the resulting figures. For example, if your floor measures 13'7'' x 16'4'', this converts to 163 x 196 inches or 18 x 21 tiles. You'll need 378 tiles, plus 5 to 10 percent more for edges, waste, etc.

Tiles are installed from the center of the room outward. Measure to find the center point of each end wall, disregarding any offsets, bays, alcoves, or other irregularities. Snap a chalk line between the two center points, having a helper hold one end of the line or securing it under a brick or other heavy object. Repeat this procedure with the two side walls. Your lines should intersect at right angles in the center of the room. Check with a square, and make any necessary adjustments.

Figure 7-6: To locate the center of a floor, find the center point of each wall in the room, then pull a chalked string taut from the mid- point to the parallel wall. Snap a straight line on the subfloor. Do the same in the other direction (*courtesy of Azrock Floor Products*).

Figure 7-7: The chalklines serve as guides for positioning loose tiles correctly on the floor (*left*). Then, if this layout brings less than a half tile to the last row nearest the baseboard, re-position the tiles. Before doing this, snap a new chalkline closer to the opposite wall—adding half of the space "leftover" from the first fitting (*right*). Then lay out the loose tiles again.

Lay a row of loose tiles along the chalk line from the center point to one side wall and another along the line to one end wall. Measure the distance between the wall and the last full tile; if this space is less than a half-tile wide, snap a new chalk line parallel to and a half-tile width from the original line, and use this as your guide (it will save a lot of cutting and fitting—plus the peculiar look—of very narrow tiles). Repeat the procedure along the perpendicular line.

Some tiles come with an adhesive backing. All you do is peel off the protective paper and press in place. With tiles requiring adhesive, work on one quarter of the floor at a time. Use a paint brush, roller, or notched trowel to spread adhesive evenly up to, but not covering, the chalk lines. Do not spread on too much adhesive; it will "bleed" through the joints between tiles. Allow the adhesive to *set* (become tacky to the touch) before tiling. Setting time will vary with the type of adhesive used; follow the manufacturer's directions.

Press the first tile into place where the chalk lines cross in center of the room. Work outward from there, butting each tile tightly and neatly against the adjoining tile or tiles. Do not slide the tiles into position, as this causes the adhesive to ooze up between tiles. Work along one end of the chalk line and lay three or four tiles; then fill out in a step-like pattern until reaching the other line bordering the room quarter. Continue in this manner until the quarter is completed, except for border tiles that must be fitted.

108

Figure 7-8: Roll or trowel a thin layer of tile adhesive on the subfloor next, working on one-fourth of the room at a time.

Remove any adhesive on the tile surface with a damp cloth or fine steel wool; then do a second quarter of the room. Continue in this manner until the room is completed.

To fit the border tiles, place a loose tile squarely on top of the last full tile closest to the wall. On top of this, place a second

109

Figure 7-9: When the subfloor (or old floor) is ready, start laying tiles as the center of the room, working from the intersection of the chalklines outward. Butt the tiles tightly and neatly in a "step" pattern along each line.

loose tile and slide it until it butts against the wall. Using the edge of the top tile as a guide, mark the tile beneath it with a sharp pencil. Cut the marked tile along this line. A pair of scissors does the job on most types of tile. For straight cuts, you can rent a tile cutter to make the job easy. Asphalt tile can be scribed with a sharp awl or knife and snapped off. Or you can heat the tile over a lamp, in an oven, or with a propane torch (carefully and lightly), and cut it with a scissors or knife. Then press the tile in place against the wall, and butt tightly against the last full tile. Slight discrepancies at the wall will be concealed by baseboard molding. It is best to remove all moldings first, but you can get an exact fit with moldings in place by using a compass or sharp dividers between the wood and the marked tile. To fit around pipes or other protrusions, make a paper pattern; then trace the outline onto the tile. Heat the tile, and cut it with a knife or shears.

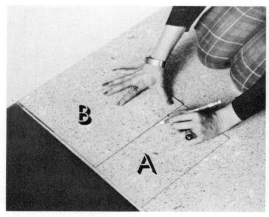 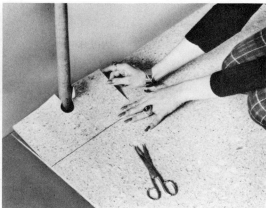

Figure 7-10: To cut and fit the wall tiles, place loose tile "A" squarely on top of the last full tile each time. Put a second loose tile "B" on top of "A" and slide it until it butts against the wall. Using the inside edge of top tile "B" as guide, mark tile "A" under it. Cut the marked tile along the pencil line with a pair of scissors or a rented tile cutter. To fit around pipes and other obstructions, make a paper pattern to fit the space exactly, then trace it onto a tile and cut it out with shears. Cut a slot on the wall side of the tile to fit it over the pipe (*courtesy of Azrock Floor Products*).

Sheet Vinyl Floors

Sheet flooring may have been the bane of do-it-yourselfers in days of yore—but no more. Once again, modern technology (and smart technologists who have come to realize where their market really is) to the rescue! New materials and new methods make the installation of so-called sheet goods as easy as putting down tiles—and in some ways easier, since the job can often be done without even using mastic.

Remove any moldings by gently prying them up from the floor and away from the wall. Remove rubber or vinyl cove-base by working one corner loose and pulling it away while breaking adhesive bond with a scraping tool. Thoroughly clean the floor with a vacuum and pick up all dirt and grit.

Using a scissors, shears, or sharp knife, cut the new sheet vinyl roughly to the shape of the room. Sketch the room first, showing counters, bays, alcoves, or other features that will affect the shape and size of the flooring. Transfer these measurements to the new sheet vinyl, and cut it 3″ larger all around. Make sure both the pattern and the new flooring are laid face up. Roll up the material with the pattern showing and tie with string.

There must be a minimum 1/8″ clearance gap between the edge of the material and each wall to allow for expansion and con-

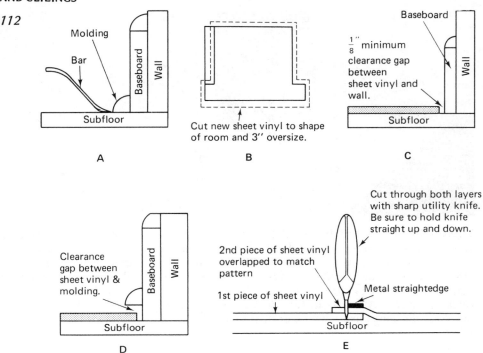

Figure 7-11: To install sheet vinyl, first remove shoe moldings along baseboard (A), then cut flooring to fit pattern; keep a 3″ overlap (B). Trim all around, leaving 1/8″ clearance between edge and basement. Re-install the molding, using scrap lumber to form clearance above the vinyl (D). Study the method for overlapping the sections (E) so the pattern matches.

traction of the underfloor. The maximum gap allowable is slightly less than the thickness of the molding that will be used to cover it.

Start at the longest and most regular wall of the room. Butt the sheet vinyl against this wall and unroll it across the room, allowing the excess material to curve up the other three walls. If your butt edge is straight with the wall, adjust the new flooring to allow the proper clearance gap. If not, straighten the edge and adjust. In some cases, where the wall is badly bowed or crooked, it may be necessary to curve the material up this starting wall and cut it to fit. Bend the material into the wall–floor joint on each of the other walls, and carefully cut it with a utility knife to allow the proper clearance. Cut slightly closer than 1/8-inch at doorways.

A clearance gap must also be allowed between the sheet vinyl and the wooden moldings to allow the walls and sub-floor to move without affecting the vinyl flooring. Wooden moldings should be re-nailed to the baseboard (not the floor) after inserting a scrap of flooring between the molding and the floor. Remove the scrap, and you will have the proper clearance. Rubber or vinyl cove-base can be cemented back to the wall without clearance. Install a metal threshold molding at doorways, fastening it to the subfloor, but not through the new sheet vinyl.

Sheet vinyl can be installed without seaming in most rooms. But even in wide rooms (over 12′) it is not difficult to seam the material. To match the pattern across the seam, it is necessary that the second piece of material be lapped over the first along the seam edge. Be sure to allow enough material in width and length to match the pattern when rough cutting.

Bring the material into the room and overlap it to match the pattern. After the pattern is matched, weight it down or tape it in place so it will not shift. Cut the flooring to fit at the three walls as before, allowing proper clearance. Using a metal straightedge as a guide, cut through both the first and second pieces of sheet vinyl in the overlapped area with a sharp utility knife. Follow a natural line in the pattern when possible. Keep the knife vertical, not leaning to the right or left. Remove the cut-off pieces, top and bottom.

Lay back one piece of sheet vinyl at the seam. Draw a pencil line on the floor along the edge of the second piece. Lay back the second piece, and spread a 6″ band of adhesive under the seam area, centered on the pencil line. If the underfloor has been waxed, sand the area lightly. Spread the adhesive with a fine notched trowel (11 notches to the inch, 1/32″ deep). Lay the sheet vinyl into the wet adhesive, and wipe it with a damp cloth to assure good contact with the adhesive. Remove the excess adhesive while still wet using water.

Carpeting

The development of synthetic shag has made carpeting a popular choice for both above- and below-grade installation (such as a basement floor) by the do-it-yourselfer. This carpeting is nylon fiber with an underside pad of foamed latex. Above the latex is a primary backing (the part that shows when the tufts of the carpet are spread apart) of woven polypropylene, which is impervious to moisture. The carpeting is available in 12 x 12-inch tiles and in 6-foot- and 12-foot-wide rolls.

To install the carpet tiles, lay out the room as for resilient tiles. Most carpet tiles have their own adhesive already applied. All you have to do is peel off the protective paper, and press the tile into position, like the adhesive-backed resilient tiles mentioned above. Fitting the borders is a simple matter of cutting the carpet with a household scissors.

Figure 7-12: Carpet tiles such as Armstrong's Sunstep are fitted and laid much like vinyl tiles, but most are self-stick and require no separate adhesive.

Roll carpeting is even more simple to put down. Just roll it out on the floor, and trim it with a heavy shears to fit along the room edges. Apply double-faced carpet tape to hold it down at door openings and to hold adjacent pieces snugly together at seams. Precision-cut factory edges butt tightly, and the shag texture hides the seams.

Figure 7-13: To install shag carpeting, begin by running a thick crayon marker around the edges of the floor at the baseboard so that a double rule is made. Next, roll out the carpet, letting it run up against the baseboard. Press the carpeting down on the marks so that they will transfer to the carpet backing. Then cut between the two lines.

Tape is not needed at the edges, but it is necessary at the seams and in doorways. Lay double-faced tape on the floor and press the carpeting down against it. The second roll butts to the first, thus concealing the seams (*courtesy of Armstrong Cork*).

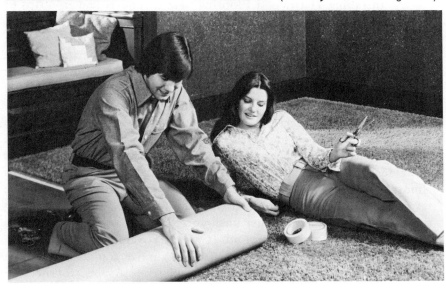

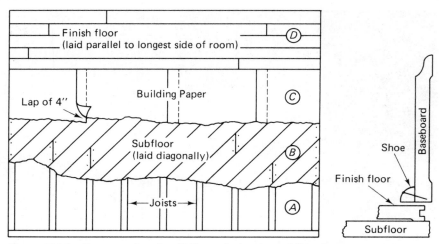

Figure 7-14: Construction details for strip hardwood flooring.

Hardwood Flooring

The popularity of area rugs is on the increase, and there are many who like the appearance of bare wood, without any rugs at all. Hardwood is subject to damage from dampness below ground level, and it is not generally recommended for basements. It also seems a bit of waste up in the attic, unless you're using it as a sitting room or apartment. The best application, for our purposes, is in a garage or porch renovation.

Installing Hardwood Flooring: Hardwood is laid in strips or parquet blocks over either plywood or tongue-and-groove sheathing. A layer of 15-pound building paper is also advised, particularly when used over concrete. (Check the manufacturer's instructions for specific recommendations.) The building paper should be placed at right angles to strip flooring, which is laid parallel to the longer dimension of the room.

Tongue-and-groove strip flooring is started 3/4" from the wall, with the groove side to the wall. The flooring is fastened with flooring nails driven diagonally 12" o.c. into the top of the tongue. Your dealer, or a rental shop, should have an automatic nailer that is almost indispensable for fast and accurate installation. Use the fasteners that are recommended with the machine. Continue nailing the strips in the same manner until you reach the other side. Leave a 3/4" expansion margin all around. It will be covered by molding.

Some parquet blocks are laid in similar tongue-and-groove fashion; others are installed with adhesive. Again, follow the manufacturer's directions.

Figure 7-15: Parquet flooring consists of glued squares made from fine strip flooring. This Hartco Foam-Tile has its own adhesive backing.

Sanding: Whether your flooring is oak (most likely)—or less popular maple, beech, birch, or pecan—the secret of success is in the finishing. Once the flooring is laid, the work has just begun.

The finishing process begins with thorough sanding. The technique to be followed from here on can also be used later for refinishing the floors when they become worn and dirty. With older floors, sanding removes stains, scratches, high spots, and just plain dirt. New flooring, although smoothly surfaced at the factory, is inevitably marked and scratched during handling and installation.

Proper floor sanding requires the use of several machines. You will need a larger sander for the larger areas, and a smaller one for edges, corners, and other tight places, plus a little hand sander and/or scraper for hard-to-reach spots.

For fine floors, most manufacturers recommend at least four sandings, although you may feel you can get away with less. In no case should you give the floors fewer than three sandings.

Start with No. 2 sandpaper and graduate to No. 1/2, No. 0, and No. 00 (see Table 7-1, page 119). For best results, another buffing with No. 00 or No. 000 assures an even smoother surface. The experts say that the final traverse should be made by hand, although it is hard to envision the average amateur (or even the hardened professional, for that matter) crawling across the floor on hands and knees after already going through four machine sandings.

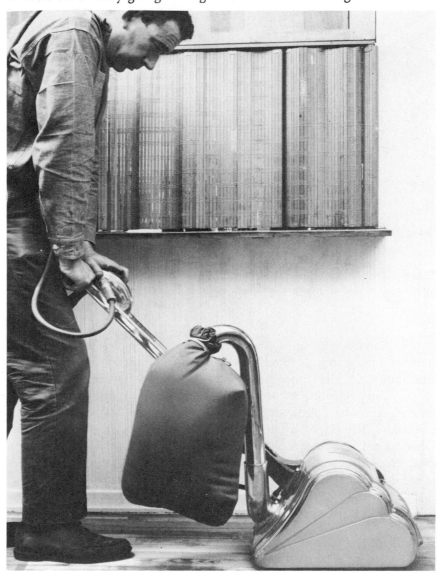

Figure 7-16: Thorough sanding is the secret of a fine floor finish. You can rent a good sander like this one at most rental outlets (*courtesy of Benjamin Moore & Company*).

Figure 7-17: Finish the floor carefully with a hand sander.

Table 7-1: CHART OF SANDING OPERATIONS FOR NEW FLOORS

FLOOR	OPERATION	CONDITION OF FLOOR	GRADE OF SANDPAPER*	
HARDWOOD Oak, Maple, Beech, Birch	First Cut	Uneven Floor	Medium-Coarse	2 (36)
		Ordinary Floor	Fine	1 (50)
	Final Sanding		Extra Fine	2/0 (100)
SOFTWOOD Pine, Fir	First Cut	Uneven Floor	Medium-Fine	1-1/2 (40)
			Fine	1 (50)
	Final Sanding	Ordinary Floor	Extra Fine	2/0 (100)

*Use closed coat sandpaper only

Figure 7-18: Clear sealer is an easy and effective floor finish.

Wood Filler: After the final sanding, by hand or otherwise, a paste wood filler is sometimes used to fill the minute crevices in oak and other woods having large pores. It gives the floor the perfectly smooth surface required for a lustrous appearance.

Filler is applied after stains, and sometimes after floor seals (check the manufacturer's instructions), but always before other finishing materials such as shellac or varnish. The filler should be allowed to dry for 24 hours before the next operation is begun. Wood filler may be colorless, or it may contain pigment to bring out the grain of the wood for greater contrast.

Types of Finish: The qualities to consider when choosing a finish for your flooring are attractive appearance, durability, ease of maintenance, and capacity for being retouched in worn spots without looking patched.

Floor Seal: Floor seal is increasingly used for residential as well as heavy-duty flooring. It differs from other finishes in this important respect: Rather than forming a surface coating, it penetrates the wood fibers, sealing them together. In effect, it becomes part of the wood itself. It wears only as the wood wears and does not chip or crack. Worn spots can be refinished without presenting a patched appearance. Floor seals are available either colorless or in colors.

Generally, floor seal is applied first across the grain and then smoothed out in the direction of the grain. A wide brush, squeegee, or wool applicator can be used. After a period of 15 minutes to 2 hours (always follow the manufacturer's directions) the excess sealing material should be wiped off with clean cloths or a rubber squeegee. For best results, the floor should then be buffed with No. 2 steel wool. One application of seal can be sufficient, but usually a second coat is recommended for recently sanded or new floors.

Varnish: Varnish presents a glossy appearance and is quite durable and resistant to stains and spots, but it will show scratches. It is difficult to patch worn spots without leaving lines of demarcation between the old and new varnish. Like most other types of finish, it is most satisfactory when properly waxed and otherwise maintained.

Precise directions for application of varnish are stated on the containers. Varnish made especially for floors is much preferred. So-called all-purpose varnish is not durable enough for use on floors.

As a rule, three coats of varnish are required when applied to bare wood, but two coats are usually adequate when wood filler has been used or when a coat of shellac has been applied first, as is sometimes the case. Cleanliness of both floor and applicator is essential to a smooth finish.

Shellac: One of the chief reasons shellac is so widely used is that it dries quickly. It is transparent and has a high gloss. It does not darken with age as quickly as varnish, but its comparatively low endurance makes it an inferior choice for flooring. Also, shellac spots rather readily if water or other liquids remain on it long.

Shellac to be used on floors should be fresh, or at least have been stored in a glass container. If it remains too long in a metal container, it may accumulate salts of iron, which discolor oak and other hardwoods containing tannin. A wide brush that covers three boards of strip flooring is the most effective and convenient. Strokes should be long and even, with laps joined smoothly.

The first coat on bare wood will dry in 15 to 20 minutes, after which the floor should be rubbed lightly with steel wool or sandpaper and then swept clean. A second coat should be applied and allowed to dry for 2 to 3 hours. Preferably, however, the floor should remain out of service overnight.

Lacquer: Lacquer gives a glossy finish with about the same durability as varnish. Because it dries so rapidly, however, lacquer requires considerable skill in application. Worn spots may be retouched with fairly good results since a new coat of lacquer dissolves the original coat. Follow the directions carefully if you use lacquer; it is difficult to apply with a brush.

Urethane: This newer finishing material, also known as *polyurethane*, is becoming increasingly popular for residential use. It provides an excellent surface with long-wearing and low-maintenance properties.

Of several different types, urethane "varnish" is a type of plastic offered by most of the nationally known paint manufacturers. Choose the product of a manufacturer in whom you have confidence, and follow the directions meticulously. It is applied much like standard varnishes.

Wax: All hardwood floors should be waxed after the finish has dried thoroughly. In some cases, two or three coats are recommended for best results. Wax not only imparts a lustrous sheen to the floor, but also forms a protective film that prevents dirt from penetrating the wood pores. When wax becomes dirty, it is usually removed and new wax applied.

Floor wax is available in two forms—paste and liquid. The liquid type recommended for hardwood floors is known as *buffing* or *spirit wax*. (Never use water-base waxes or cleaners on wood.) Considered about equal in performance, both paste and liquid are applied in much the same manner. Usually the wax is mopped on with a cloth and then polished after an interval of 15 to 30 minutes with a soft cloth, a weighted floor brush, or an electric polisher. The latter eliminates a great deal of labor and does an excellent job. Some electric polishers apply the wax and polish it in the same operation. Power-driven polishing machines, as well as sanding and buffing machines, can be rented in most rental stores.

Moldings

You will probably want to use wood baseboard molding along the bottom of the walls. This should be applied after both walls and floor have been installed. The baseboard is usually trimmed with small *shoe moldings*, which are nailed to the baseboard and not the flooring. Use 6d finishing nails for baseboard molding and 4d for shoe molding.

FINISHING THE CEILING

Few people remember who did the floor of the Sistine Chapel, but everybody knows that the incomparable Michelangelo painted that great ceiling. During those golden centuries of building on the grand scale, ceiling design was of the utmost artistic importance. But then pragmatic production techniques made it into a flat, sterile surface.

Now it would appear the the pendulum is swinging back—a trend not only welcomed but also probably inspired by the do-it-yourselfer. Modern ceiling products designed specifically for installation by the amateur are relatively low in cost, easy to install, and handsome to view.

For the attic, basement, or other finishing-off project, the choice usually narrows down to tiles or a suspended grid system. Wood or plastic paneling is another excellent selection and can produce a very dramatic effect—but it can also become tiresome. Each offers certain advantages that Michelangelo never even heard of.

For ground-level rooms, gypsum wallboard is often the choice, although tiles are probably easier to install. Suspended systems are an excellent choice for rooms with high ceilings. Lowering the headroom also saves heating and cooling costs.

Tiles are stapled or glued over an existing ceiling or to furring strips nailed to the ceiling joists. Suspended panels hang from the joists on wires or clips, and are easily removed for servicing of pipes and cables overhead. Both tiles and suspended panels can be installed so that the joints become decorative elements in the ceiling. Both are also available in types that conceal the joints so that the finished ceiling looks like a one-piece installation. And, perhaps most important for a family room situation, both are available as acoustical elements that work to keep a large percentage of the noise that is generated in the room *inside* the room.

Figure 7-19: When tile is to be affixed to a new ceiling, the most efficient method is to staple it directly to furring strips (*courtest of Armstrong Cork*).

By definition, family and recreation rooms are where the family gathers to relax and have a good time. People and fun, however, add up to noise. An acoustical ceiling helps keep the noise under control without dampening any of the enjoyment. It can actually absorb much of the sound, while preventing the remainder from spreading to quiet areas upstairs. Teen-agers can be entertaining their friends in the family room while their parents relax in more quiet pursuits directly above.

The denser the composition of the tile or suspended panel, the better it will keep sound from spreading to other areas. The densest acoustical tiles are of mineral fiber or wood fiber. Other materials, such as glass fiber, are more porous and allow the sound to pass through more easily. The sound absorbency of acoustical tile is indicated by its *noise reduction coefficient* rating, or NRC, which needn't be as mysterious as it sounds. The rating number is simply the percentage of sound striking the surface of the tile that will be absorbed. A spread of more than 10 NRC points (for example, a 0.50 tile compared to a 0.70 tile) indicates a definite edge in sound absorption for the higher-rated product. A narrower gap is more difficult for the ear to detect.

If it all sounds too scientific to *your* ear, just remember to specify acoustical tile for your family room ceiling. The slight extra cost will be one of the best investments in peace and quiet that you've ever made.

Figure 7-20: To install tile over an old ceiling, brush five dabs of cement on each; then slide it into position (*courtesy of Armstrong Cork*).

Ceiling Tiles

The most common size ceiling tiles are 12″ square; 12 x 24-, 16 x 16-, and 16 x 32-inch tiles are also available in some types. In most installations, the tiles are stapled to 1 x 3 furring strips.

Unlike floor tiles, ceiling tile installation is started in a corner of the room. Like floor tiles, a ceiling has a better appearance if border tiles are the same width on opposite sides of the room, and are as large as possible. Unlike floor tiles, ceiling tiles can't be laid out for a "dry run." To determine border tile width for the *long* walls of your family room, measure one of the *short* walls. If it is not an exact number of feet, add 12″ (assuming you are using 12″ tiles) to the inches left over; then divide the number of inches by two. This is the width of the border tiles for the long walls.

Example:

short wall	12′8″
extra inches	8″
plus	12″
divided by	2) 20″
border tile	10″

Border tiles for the *short* walls are figured by the same procedure.

Example:

long wall	18′4″
extra inches	4″
plus	12″
divided by	2) 16″
border tile	8″

Furring the Ceiling: Furring strips are nailed across the joists; it is essential that the first two strips be carefully placed so that the border tiles are properly aligned. Nail the first strip flush against the wall at right angles to the joists, driving an 8d nail into each joist. The second furring strip is placed parallel to the first at a distance determined by the border tile width from the wall. For example, add on 1/2″ for the stapling flange to the 10″ border tile width of our example. The center of the second furring strip should be 10-1/2″ from the wall (*not* from the first furring strip). With the second strip nailed in place, work across the ceiling, nailing each succeeding strip 12″ from center to center. When you reach the opposite wall, the next to last strip should automatically be in the right position (unless your measurements somehow went awry). The final strip is placed flush against the wall, just as the first one. With all strips nailed up, make sure they are level by checking them with a long straightedge. Correct any unevenness by driving thin wood shims between strips and joists.

Where pipes or cables project more than 3/4" but not more than 1-1/2" below the ceiling joists, install double furring strips over the whole ceiling, rather than just around the projections. The first series of furring strips can be spaced 24" o.c. across the joists. The second set is then applied perpendicular to the first, spaced as described above.

Pipes or ducts that project below the ceiling line should be boxed in with 2 x 2 framing before the ceiling is installed. When the tiles are in place, wood corner moldings provide finished edges.

Installing Ceiling Tile: The first tile is the most crucial. Snap a chalk line down the center of the full length of the second furring strip. In our example, this would be 10-1/2" from the wall—the width of the border tile plus flange. Snap a second chalk line across the furring strips. Again using the example above, the short wall border tiles measure 8"; add 1/2" for the flange—the second chalk line should be 8-1/2" from the wall. This line must be at an exact right angle to the first line; check it with a carpenter's square before snapping the line.

Now comes the easy part. Measure and cut each border tile individually. Remove the tongue edge and leave the flanges for stapling; include the flange in your measurement. Cut the tiles face up with a sharp utility knife.

The first tile is the corner tile. Align its flange edges with both guidelines, and staple it in place through the flanges. The second tile runs along the border parallel to the furring strips. Slide it into the first tile; it should fit snugly, but do not force the tiles tightly together. Align the flange with the guideline and staple. The third tile runs along the border across the furring strips. Slide it into the first, align it with the guideline, and staple. Work your way outward across the ceiling, installing border tiles at each end. When you reach the opposite wall, cut each border tile individually and staple each to the outside surface. And before you know it, you've got a ceiling! All that's left is nailing up the molding.

A Suspended Ceiling

The one big advantage of a suspended ceiling system is that it can be installed at whatever height is necessary to conceal pipes, ducts, and whatever else clutters the upper levels of a basement or other room. The disadvantage is that many rooms—particularly basements where such ceilings are most useful—just do not have enough headroom to sacrifice what is necessary for such an installation. To work properly, a suspended ceiling must be at least three inches below the joists, ducts, pipes, and other obstructions. (Some systems can be installed directly to the joists, but then they are no longer truly suspended.)

If you have enough overhead room, a suspended ceiling is fast and easy to install. The system will give you a ceiling line unbroken by protrusions of boxed-in ducts and pipes; yet it still allows easy access to these utilities for servicing—simply lift out the ceiling panel below them. You can also provide recessed lighting with fluorescent fixtures installed above translucent panels in selected areas of the room—or in the whole ceiling if you wish. (All-translucent ceilings are a bit much except in very small rooms.) To prevent "hot spots," use fixtures especially designed for these ceilings. Otherwise, provide reflectors above the fluorescent tubes, with adequate space as recommended by the manufacturer.

Figure 7-21:   The suspended ceiling in this attractive basement allowed the do-it-yourselfer to work around pipes and wiring without involved "boxing."

Figure 7-22: Fluorescent fixtures fit nicely into a suspended grid and provide recessed lighting that can be located where you want it.

Suspended ceiling panels are available in a wide variety of patterns and sizes—2 x 2-foot and 2 x 4-foot panels are the most common. The suspension systems also vary, depending on the manufacturer. For example, some use a gridwork hung on wires; others use clips. Specific instructions accompany the system that you purchase. In general, the job goes as follows.

First, make an accurate sketch of the ceiling, noting the locations of pipes, heating ducts, lights, and the like. This will help you plan the installation, and will also be an aid later on when you need access to these utilities for servicing. Determine what type of lighting fixtures you want to install (if any) and where they will be located. These are best installed before you do the ceiling.

Determine the exact height of the new ceiling, and snap a

Figure 7-23: Standard suspended ceilings like this one use 2 × 4-foot grids. The panels are tipped in as shown.

chalk line at that height on all walls of the room (make sure that these lines are level). Fasten the wall molding (usually an L-shaped metal fitting) to each wall, aligning it with the chalk line. The molding should be nailed to every stud. If a window extends above the new ceiling height, box it in with a valance of 3/4″ lumber nailed to the joists at the same height as the chalk line. Then nail the wall molding around the bottom edge of the valance.

The main supporting runners are installed at right angles to the joists. Chalk lines are snapped across the joists (the locations of these lines will depend on the size of the panels and the size of your room); then clips or screw eyes and wires are fastened at intervals along these lines. The main runners are suspended from these clips or wires, resting on the wall molding at each end.

Figure 7-24: Armstrong's new "Integrid" suspended system uses sliding "tee" runners which hook into special slots in leading edge of each tile. Layouts are not necessary.

With all main runners secured, the panels are set in place on the runners. Panels are separated from one another by cross runners that rest on the main runners. Border panels are cut to fit using a sharp utility knife. The border tiles rest on the wall molding and the adjacent main runner.

Figure 7-25: Finished Integrid ceiling looks as if it were installed all in one piece since the seams are practically invisible.

Elements of Electricity

8

Almost any kind of renovation job discussed here involves at least a smattering of electrical work. Electricity is sort of the opposite of the weather. Nobody understands it, but everybody does something with it. Flip a switch and the light goes on. Plug in an appliance and it goes to work. Electricity cooks, sews, washes, drys, heats, cools, lights, irons, cleans, entertains, communicates, warns, does dishes, mixes, blends, disposes of garbage, compacts trash, shaves whiskers, and brushes teeth.

Yet, almost everybody is afraid of it—and with good reason. Electricity is a wonderful servant, but a nasty master. It can burn, maim, and even kill. Because of these potential dangers, most municipalities have statutes forbidding do-it-yourself wiring, or requiring that any person attempting such jobs first obtain a building permit and then have the wiring approved by a licensed electrician and/or an official inspector.

DO IT YOURSELF?

Most literature on this subject warns against do-it-yourself wiring, while at the same time giving directions for doing it. We'd like to shy away from such hypocrisy. There are many people who are frightened to death by the thought of installing a new light fixture, and if that's how you are, then you probably shouldn't try electrical work. You should read on, though, to cure yourself of this fear. If, however, you are simply concerned about your safety, plus violations of the building codes, insurance "laws," and plain common sense, rest assured that you *can* perform most home wiring jobs as long as you read and work carefully, and comply with your local building codes. Here we'll show you how to do the easier jobs and warn you away from the dangerous ones.

The intelligent way to approach electrical work is to avoid it if you are really apprehensive—although it won't hurt to learn about it. After you've read the *entire* chapter, evaluate the job to be done and re-read the specific instructions for each kind of installation. If you think you can do it, give it a try. But do a little more reading first. Sears has an excellent inexpensive booklet on the subject. Or if you are more interested in theory, etc., John Doyle's *An Introduction to Electrical Wiring* (Reston, Va.: Reston Publishing Company, Inc., 1975) is a good text.

Start with the easy work, like wiring the boxes, and don't hook up to the hot stuff until you're sure you know what you're doing. A neon tester is an inexpensive device to check your work without danger to yourself or others.

THE BASICS

Before you even touch an electrical wire, you should have an understanding of basic electrical principles. You don't have to become an electrical engineer, but you should have a solid knowledge of what electricity does, even if you don't understand why.

Always be sure that both you and/or your electrician use materials and installation techniques in accordance with the requirements of your local utility company, municipal and state codes and regulations, plus the National Electric Code. The latter Code is a set of rules approved by the National Board of Fire Underwriters to serve as a guide to wiring safety. All receptacles, switches, fixtures, wires, and other material should bear the stamp of approval by Underwriters' Laboratories (UL), but you should also realize that this means only that the fixture has passed *minimum* requirements. It pays to use quality materials.

Before you do anything, it is wise to define terms:
* An *ampere (amp)* is the measure of the quantity of electric current that flows past a given point in a given time.
* *Voltage*—measured in *volts (V)*—is the pressure that starts an electric current and keeps it moving.
* *Wattage*—measured in *watts (W)*—tells you how much

electricity is being used at a given point. Watts are determined by multiplying the amperes by the volts.

* A *kilowatt (kw)* is 1,000 watts; a *kilowatt-hour (kw-h)* is 1,000 watts used for one hour.
* *Horsepower (hp)* is a rating of power used on some household appliances. One horsepower equals 746 watts.
* A *circuit* is the wire or wires through which electricity flows from the supply point to the point of use and back.

HOW ELECTRICITY WORKS

The best way to understand electricity is to think of it as water being carried to various parts of your house through water pipes. The pipes are the wiring. And power is what keeps it going. The power is piped into your home, and the electrical current is separated at a fuse box or circuit breaker box into smaller wires or branch circuits that flow throughout the house. Again like water pipes, the branch circuits are designed to carry greater or lesser amounts of current, according to the demands to be made upon it. For example, more power is required for an electric washer than for a table lamp, and the circuits are wired accordingly (see Table 8-1).

Whenever more current is drawn through a circuit than it is designed to carry, there will be trouble. Wires heat up, upsetting the whole system. Voltages drop, and appliances starve and begin to overheat. Heat burns insulation, wastes electricity, eventually burns out motors, and causes appliance failure.

Older electrical systems, installed primarily to provide power for lighting, often give only 30-amp, 120-volt service, for a maximum of 3,600 watts. Today, with such appliances as air conditioners, heaters, irons, and even toasters requiring 1,000 watts or more each, such systems are dangerously inadequate.

A modern system should be 120/240-volts with no less than 100-amp service, making 24,000 watts available. This type of system provides adequate power for separate circuits serving 240-volt appliances like stoves, clothes dryers, and heavy-duty air conditioners.

WIRING DEVICES

Copper wire is used to conduct current to receptacles throughout the house. The diameter of the wire determines the amount of current that can be carried, just as the size of a water pipe determines water flow. Most home circuits use 12 or 14 gage wire (about 1/16 inch in diameter); 16 and 18 gage wire is used for doorbells, intercoms, and similar devices. The lower the number, the thicker and more powerful the wire. Stranded wire, called *lamp cord*, is used for most lamp and small appliance connections.

Various materials are used as insulation on the copper wire. For special applications, outdoors, and in wet locations, heat- and moisture-resistant insulations are available.

Cable, used for most home circuits, consists of two or more insulated wires grouped inside a covering. The two most common types are *BX* (flexible steel armored cable) and *Romex* (nonmetallic sheathed cable). Romex is slightly cheaper, lighter, more flexible, and easier to work with. The steel armor on BX, although more difficult to cut, gives it a continuous ground and protects the wires inside from damage. Some communities will allow the use of only BX cable. Romex, however, is perfectly safe for virtually all do-it-yourself projects.

Both BX and Romex normally carry two or three wires and are designated according to the number and size of these wires. A cable with two 14-gage wires is called 14-2; three-wire cables are called 14-3 or 12-3.

In two-wire cable, one wire has black insulation; this is the "hot" wire. The neutral or "ground" wire has white insulation for identification. In three-wire cable, the third wire (also "hot") has red insulation or none at all. Most new installations also have a true grounding wire that carries no current at all and simply serves to shunt dangerous shorts and appliance defects away from people. This is generally bare or covered with green insulation.

Before installing cable in a circuit, the sheathing must be removed where connections are to be made. The metal spiral of BX cable is best cut with a hacksaw; take care not to cut through the wires, though. To prepare nonmetallic sheathed cable, or Romex, make a knife cut in the sheathing parallel to and between the wires, again being careful not to cut into the wires or the insulation. Pull the sheathing back and cut it off.

With the sheathing off (about 6 inches for most connections), peel the paper wrapping from the wires. Using a sharp knife or special wire stripper, cut through the insulation about 1 inch from the end of each wire. Your cut should be slanted toward the end, taking care not to nick the copper. Strip off all the insulating material. The cable is now ready to be connected (see page 135).

Where extra protection for wiring is needed, conduit (pipe) is used. Rigid conduit looks very much like water pipe, and is cut and threaded in the same way. Thin-wall conduit is much lighter than the

Right way   Wrong way

Cut the wires to be spliced and remove the insulation by cutting at a slant, as in sharpening a pencil. Expose $\frac{1}{2}$" of copper conductor. Be sure to remove all the insulation, but not the tin coating which helps in soldering.

Start splice   Finish splice

To splice wires together, just remove about 3 inches of insulation from each wire. Next cross the wires about 1 inch from the insulation; Then make 6 to 8 turnings, using fingers and pliers.

Apply solder to the splice. So the solder will flow easier, first coat the wires with electric soldering paste. Then heat the wires with the iron until the solder melts and flows into every crevice.

Right way   Wrong way

Connections at screw terminals are made by bending the end of the metal wire into a loop to fit around screw. Be sure to attach loop in direction in which screw turns when tightening — as illustrated above on the left.

Combination wire cutter and stripper makes a handy tool. It cuts and strips clean all sizes of solid or stranded copper wire. Use it also for looping wires under screws.

Tap splices are used to connect the end of one wire at a point on a continuous wire. Use only if there is no pull on the tapped wire. Bare and clean the tap wire, then wrap it around continuous wire. Solder and tape.

Plastic tape does a faster, neater, cleaner job than rubber and friction tape. Easier to handle, it takes less space in boxes. It does the work of both rubber and friction tape and is water-proof and acid-proof.

Solderless connectors eliminate the need for soldering joints. They are made of insulating material so the wires need not be taped; and short circuits can't occur. Just screw the connector over the wires as shown above.

Figure 8-1: Mastery of basic wiring techniques includes a good working knowledge of the cutting, taping, splicing, tapping, and soldering or connecting methods shown in the eight diagrams above.

To splice is to join the ends of 2 wires together. A tap is the joining of a wire at right angles to a continuous wire. To make splices and taps as strong as a continuous piece of wire, the job must be done well; otherwise trouble will result.

To make a good connection, the wires must be bright and clean when brought together. The connection must be tight, well fastened with solder or solderless connectors and covered with tape. In this way, the wire is as well insulated as originally.

Remember: You must solder all splices and taps *except* where solderless connectors are used (*courtesy of Sears, Roebuck & Company*).

rigid and cannot be threaded; special fittings are used to couple joints and to connect the conduit to outlet boxes.

Boxes must be used wherever a cable terminates or is joined to another cable. These metal boxes come in a variety of sizes and shapes to suit various purposes. Outlet boxes are usually octagonal, square, or round, with the rectangular type most common. *Knockout holes* are provided for the entry of wires; connectors with locknuts or clamps secure the cable firmly. Fitted with a blank cover, an outlet box serves as a junction box, where wires are joined. (This type is usually octagonal.) Never attempt to join circuit wires outside a box. This is very dangerous, as well as being a serious violation of the National Electric Code. Outlet boxes are also used for ceiling fixtures, and they may be fitted with switches or receptacles for plug-in lamps and appliances.

In-wall switches and receptacles are sometimes installed in special switch boxes. These are attached to wall studs or other framing members. Like outlet boxes, they have a number of knockout holes to permit wires to enter from a variety of directions. The wires are then attached to one or more switches or receptacles that are, in turn, screwed into place and covered with faceplates.

YOUR HOME'S ELECTRICAL CIRCUITS

Whether you intend to do your own work or not, if new wiring is to be part of a remodeling project, you should first familiarize yourself with the existing circuits. Basically, there are three types of circuits.

* *General purpose circuits* are used for most receptacle outlets, lighting, and low-wattage outlets. They are usually wired with #14 cable and are fused at 15 amps maximum. As a rule of thumb, there should be one general purpose circuit for each 500 square feet of floor area. Newer houses usually have #12 wiring which is now the recommended minimum in most codes.
* *Special appliance circuits* are used for receptacle outlets in the kitchen, dining room, pantry, breakfast room, and laundry. They use #12 wire and 20-amp fuses.
* *Individual appliance circuits* are provided for such high-wattage appliances as ranges, oil burners, water heaters, automatic washers, dryers, and some workshop equipment. Cable size depends on the load required by the appliance.

It is quite simple to determine the setup of your present electrical system, which circuits may be overtaxed, and which ones

Table 8-1: WATTAGE RATINGS OF STANDARD APPLIANCES

Appliance	Typical Wattage	Appliance	Typical Wattage
Air conditioner	1100	Ironer	1650
Attic fan	400	Lamps, each bulb	40-100
Automatic toaster	1200	Mechanism for fuel-fired	
Automatic washer	700	heating plant	800
Broiler	1000	Mixer	100
Built-in ventilating fan	400	Oil burner	250
Coffee maker	1000	Portable fan	100
Egg cooker	600	Portable heater	1650
Deep fryer	1320	Radio	100
Dehumidifier	350	Ranges, Electric	8000
Dishwasher-Disposer	1500	Refrigerator	200
Dry iron or Steam iron	1000	Room cooler	600
Electric blankets	200	Rotisserie	1380
Electric clock	2	Roaster	1380
Clothes dryer	4500	Sandwich grill	1320
Freezer	350	TV, Black-and-White	350
Fluorescent lights		Vacuum cleaner	300
(each tube)	15-40	Ventilating fan	400
Griddle	1000	Waffle iron	1320
Hair dryer	100	Waste disposer	500
Heat or Sun lamp	300	Water heater	2500
Hot plate	1500	Water pump	700

may not be working up to capacity and can be extended. First, turn on all the lights, including those plugged into receptacles. Then turn off the main switch or breaker at the service entrance and remove one fuse (or trip the handle of a circuit breaker to the *off* position if your system does not have fuses). Don't remove fuses while the power is on. You could get a severe shock.

With the fuse removed, turn the main switch on. Now make a list of all the outlets in the house where the lights are out. Check receptacles that are not in use with a neon tester, night-light plug, or small lamp. Also check all appliances. Especially in older homes, some appliances may be on a general purpose circuit. This is a dangerous situation and is generally forbidden by the National Electric Code.

When your list for the circuit is complete, shut off the main switch again, replace the fuse, and remove another one. Repeat the procedure until all the circuits have been checked. When you know which outlets are being carried by each circuit, figure how much power is demanded of each circuit. Add up the wattages at each

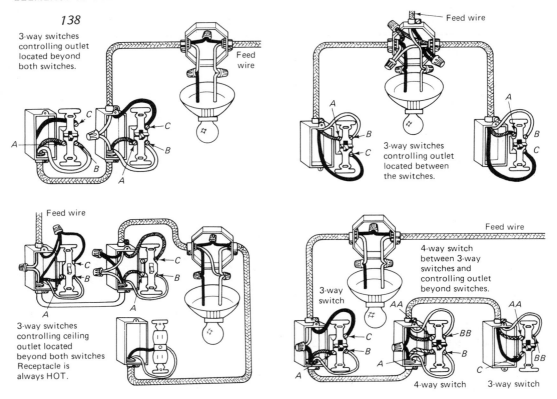

3-way switches controlling outlet located beyond both switches.

Feed wire

Feed wire

3-way switches controlling outlet located between the switches.

Feed wire

3-way switches controlling ceiling outlet located beyond both switches Receptacle is always HOT.

Feed wire

4-way switch between 3-way switches and controlling outlet beyond switches.

3-way switch

4-way switch   3-way switch

Figure 8-2: Switches are rather complicated to install, but one of the situations outlined above should apply to your problem. The diagrams apply to three- and four-way switches.

outlet. Wattage is given on light bulbs and most appliances, or refer to Table 8-1. The total will permit you to evaluate the power load on each circuit.

By checking the chart, you can see clearly how well your present electrical system is doing the job. A 15-amp, 120-volt circuit delivers 1,800 watts. If you expect it to light a 150-watt ceiling fixture while curling your hair (720 watts) in front of the television set (300 watts) and basking in the warmth of a portable heater (1200 watts), you are asking for trouble—about 570 watts worth, a very dangerous overload.

You might be tempted to replace the 15-amp fuse in such a circuit with a 20-amp fuse, thus theoretically (or at least mathematically) raising the capacity of the circuit to 2,400 watts, enough to accommodate all the aforementioned equipment with a little to spare. *Never give in to this temptation!* By routing more electricity through a circuit than it is designed to carry, you run a very serious danger of overheating wires and connections, damaging insulation, and ultimately short-circuiting the system.

On the other hand, you may find some circuits that are loafing along, doing no more than occasionally lighting a few table lamps. If your remodeling job calls for only a few outlets, use these circuits. It may also be possible to shift some of the load from the overworked circuits to the underutilized ones, simply by shifting the plugs of lamps, the stereo set, fans, and the like. If this is impractical, you may be able to add more outlets to the lazy circuits to help their hardworking brothers.

In calculating the capacities of your circuits, however, do not try to squeeze the last watt out of each one. Leave a small margin for safety. Remember, too, that motor-driven appliances, such as fans, vacuum cleaners, refrigerators, blenders, can openers, hair dryers, and workshop tools, consume much more than their normal power for a few seconds after they are started. If two or three such appliances are started at the same time on a circuit that is already being used to full capacity, a fuse will probably blow.

Adding to an Existing Circuit

There is no special trick involved in adding a new outlet or two to an existing circuit. Basically, you open a junction box or receptacle box on the circuit, and attach new wires. In a junction box, splice black wires together and white wires together, twisting them into a "pigtail" with a pair of pliers. Apply rosin-core solder to the splices, and cover them completely with electrical tape. Or you can eliminate the solder-and-tape method by covering the splices with solderless connectors, called *wire nuts*. Crimp-type solderless connectors are also available. When attaching wires to an existing receptacle the black wire goes to the brass screw, the white wire to the "silver" (zinc) screw. Bend the exposed ends of the wires into a loop, place them over the screws, squeeze with long-nose pliers, and tighten the screws.

Now run the wires to a new box through the hole knocked out on the appropriate side, connect them to a receptacle, and screw the receptacle to the box. That is all there is to it—almost.

The tricky part lies in getting the wires from the old outlet to the new. If you are working in new construction, such as a basement or attic partition, it is a simple matter to drill holes through the framing studs before covering them with gypsumboard or paneling, and then thread the cable through. In some situations (for example, a

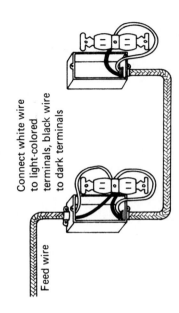

Connect white wire
to light-colored
terminals, black wire
to dark terminals

Feed wire

To add new convenience outlets beyond the old convenience outlets

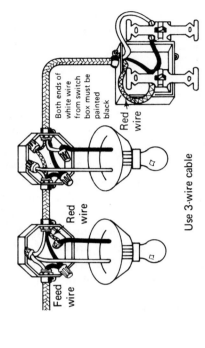

Both ends of
white wire
from switch
box must be
painted
black

Red
wire

Red
wire

Feed
wire

Use 3-wire cable

To install one new ceiling outlet and two new switch outlets
from an existing ceiling outlet

Paint white wire
black at switch
& at fixture

Feed wire

To add a wall switch to control a ceiling light in middle of run

Feed wire

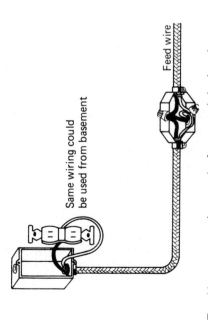

Same wiring could
be used from basement

To add a new convenience outlet from an existing junction
box

Pull chain light OR Duplex receptacle

Red wire

Feed wire

To install two ceiling lights on same line: one controlled by a switch

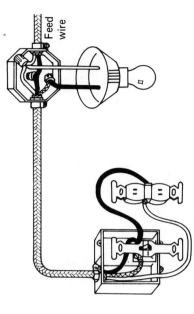

Feed wire

To add a switch and convenience outlet in one outlet box beyond existing ceiling light

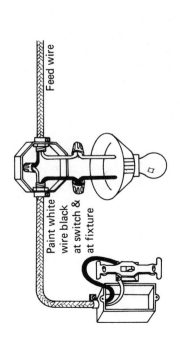

Feed wire

Paint white wire black at switch & at fixture

To add a wall switch to control ceiling light at the end of the run

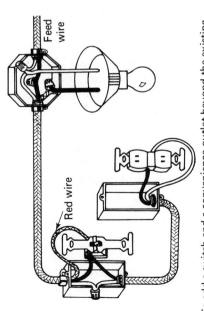

Feed wire

Red wire

To add a switch and a convenience outlet beyond the existing ceiling light

Figure 8-3: These diagrams show how to install single-switch controls for additional outlets.

living room wall backing on a garage wall), the framing may be covered on one side only, with studs exposed on the other. Here again, holes are drilled through the studs and the cable pulled through. To get wire through old construction, a steel "fish" tape is used to find an open route, then it is hooked to the wiring and pulled through to the new outlet.

Adding a Complete Circuit

If you have just a couple of outlets or lighting fixtures, you should be able to find an underloaded existing circuit to tie into. Larger rooms, however, or any room where you contemplate use of an air conditioner, wall heater, power tools, or any appliance with a heating element, will demand the addition of a complete new circuit. The fuse or circuit breaker box, the point of origin for the circuit, is a risky place for the novice do-it-yourselfer, but this doesn't necessarily mean that you have to hire an electrician to do the entire job. You can install new breakers in the empty "stalls" left in most modern boxes. Just make sure that the main power disconnect is *off.*

One possible compromise in this situation is to hire an electrician to do the hookup for you, but install all the wiring yourself. If you do your part first, then the electrician can check your work and make sure it's safe.

There is nothing very special about doing the wiring. Just follow the precepts outlined above and the manufacturers' instructions. You'll no doubt be working with new partitions, so simply nail boxes to the framing, drill holes through the centers of your studs or joists, run the wires to each receptacle, and attach them.

When you buy a switch, outlet, or whatever, the wiring diagrams should be on the device. That, plus the drawings and directions here, should be adequate for any minor job. Three-way switches, which are common for a basement stairway, can be tricky, but study the drawings carefully, and you should be able to manage it. However, you will need special switches with three terminals and a three-wire line (not counting the bare ground).

Heating the New Space

9

High energy costs notwithstanding, most of us have become too accustomed to modern creature comforts to be willing to rough it in a new but unheated bedroom, family room, or whatever. In fact, it is highly likely that air conditioning, as well as heating, will be part of your scheme.

These comfort considerations should figure early in your expansion planning. When the jobs are actually done—whether during the framing stage of the new room or later on when the walls are in place—will be determined by the method of heating (and air conditioning, if that is in the program) that you decide on.

HEATING SYSTEM CAPACITY

The furnace that currently heats your home (whether hot-air or hot-water, oil- or gas-fired) may be large enough to take on the added task of heating the new room. *May* be. Often, a contractor will install a furnace with more capacity than is needed in order to provide for expansion. But if your furnace is already working at full tilt to heat your present house, you will be inviting trouble and aggravation by asking it to do more—the heat that goes to the new room will have to come from somewhere else.

There are complicated formulas that are used to determine heating needs in relation to furnace capacities. But unless you are a heating engineer or a higher mathematician, you are better off leaving these to the experts. If you are in doubt about whether the unit can handle the extra load, seek advice from your fuel dealer or from the utility that supplies you with gas or electricity.

If you live in a house that is uninsulated or underinsulated, you may be able to, in effect, increase the capacity of the present furnace by insulating not only the new area but also the old area. If the furnace doesn't have to work as hard heating the present house, it may be able to take on the additional assignment without much trouble.

ADDING TO A HOT-WATER SYSTEM

Residential hot-water heating is either a one- or a two-pipe system. The one-pipe system uses a single supply pipe that circles the basement and returns to the boiler, with smaller pipes branching off this main to feed radiators or convectors in the rooms throughout the house. Provided that the capacity of the furnace and the main is large enough, you can tap into the main to supply additional radiators or convectors for rooms at the first floor level and above (for heating basement rooms, see below).

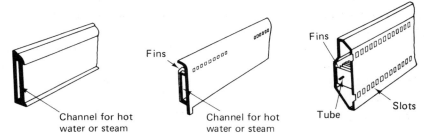

Figure 9-1: Various types of radiators can be added to your present hot water system to heat first- and second-floor rooms—if the system has the capacity. These three are among the most efficient and are usually available in most areas.

In most cases, the main line will be copper pipe. Close a shutoff valve somewhere behind the area to be tapped, and drain the line. Use a hacksaw or tubing cutter to cut through the pipe. File off any burrs at the cut, and clean the end of the pipe with steel wool. Add a *tee* to reconnect the pipe and to accommodate new fittings as necessary to reach the location of the new radiator. For a second floor room, you will probably have to drill holes from the basement through the subflooring and floor plate, and from the attic

through the top plate, to allow the pipe to be brought up through a
first floor wall. This may require lifting some floorboards in the attic;
make sure you do the roughing-in for the heating early in the framing
stage.

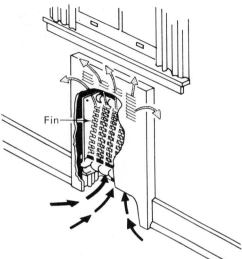

Fin

Figure 9-2: Convectors for hot water heating can either be installed against a wall or recessed in it as shown here at the right.

Copper piping is assembled by *sweating* the joints. With a little
practice, you will be able to make perfect joints. Make sure that both
the ends of the pipe and the inside of the fitting to be connected are
clean by wiping them with emery cloth. Apply a thin film of
soldering flux to both the end of the pipe and the inside of the
fitting. Place the fitting on the pipe, and twist it slightly to spread
the flux evenly. Push the two pieces tightly together. Use a propane
torch to heat the fitting at the joint. When the flux begins to bubble,
back off the torch and hold the solder to the joint, allowing it to
flow into the joint by capillary action. Wipe off the excess with a rag,
and the job is done. Be very careful with the torch flame when you
are soldering near wood, such as joists and subflooring. If you must
direct the flame near wood, protect the area with asbestos sheeting.

In a one-pipe hot-water system, radiators must be several
inches above the main to function properly. For this reason, they are
not practical for heating the basement, where overhead room is
usually minimal. A simple solution is to install *heat fins*. These fins,
usually of aluminum, are installed in clusters over the main, and do a
good job of radiating heat. They are held in place by sheet metal
screws or tabs and can be concealed behind perforated sheet
aluminum or similar material.

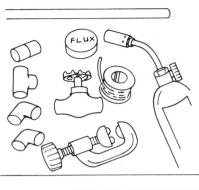

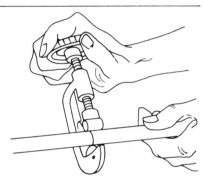

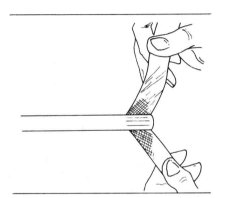

Figure 9-3: Technique for connecting fittings to copper pipe: assemble tools and materials, including a tube cutter, solder, flux, propane torch and fittings (*left*). Cut the pipe with a tube cutter (*below, left*) or hacksaw; then clean the pipe end with steel wool or emery cloth (*below*). Clean the inside of the fitting also.

In a two-pipe system, there are both supply and return lines. In this system, radiators can be cut in below the main line, so that they can be installed in basement rooms as well as above the main line. However, a return line must be provided, and the radiator return outlet must be above the boiler water line. Heat fins can also be used with this system.

ADDING TO A HOT-AIR SYSTEM

Again, make sure that the furnace is adequate for the task you are assigning it. Most modern hot-air furnaces are the forced circulation type, with a fan or blower to push the heated air throughout the system and to draw cold air from the various rooms for reheating. Another type, the gravity furnace, works on the principle that warm air rises because it is lighter than cold air, and utilizes gravity to deliver the heated air through pipes and ducts. Gravity furnaces, usually characterized by an octopus-like maze of

Figure 9-3 (*cont.*): Then apply a thin film of flux to the end of the pipe (*right*). Place each fitting on the pipe (*below*) and rotate it slightly to spread flux evenly. Hold the solder to the joint and heat each fitting—NOT the solder (*below, right*). The solder will flow into the joints by capillary action and seal the connections, thus "sweating" the copper pipe and the fittings together as they cool.

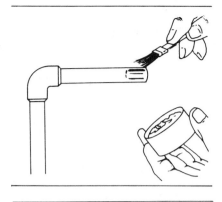

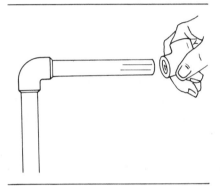

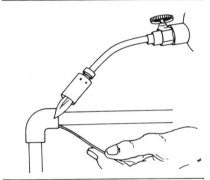

pipes in the basement, are seldom seen today, although you may have one in a vintage home, and if it is still in reasonable operating shape, you may be able to use it to heat your new room or rooms.

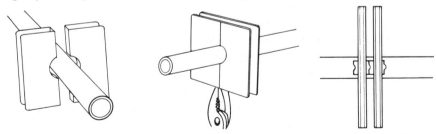

Figure 9-4: Heat fins can often be installed in the basement over the main hot water line. A 3-foot cluster of fins will heat a fair-sized room.

To tap into a gravity system, you first have to find an open space on the *plenum*—the sheet metal "bonnet" that sits on top of the furnace and out of which all those pipes start their journeys. For

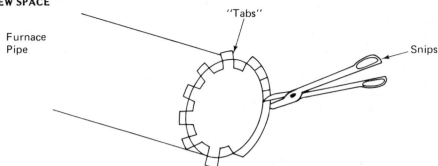

Furnace
Pipe

"Tabs"

Snips

Figure 9-5: Attach a new pipe or fitting to a sheet metal plenum or the duct for a hot air furnace by cutting notches in the end of the pipe, and then bending up every other tab outside the plenum. Fit the remainder of the tabs inside it.

first- and second-floor heating, 8″ or 9″ pipe is usually used. With the pipe as a pattern, draw a pencil outline on the plenum. Inside the outline, make a gash in the metal by hitting a cold chisel or an old screwdriver with a hammer. Insert the point of a compound-action or aviation snips (it may sound like a formidable tool, but it can be bought in any hardware store, and is a valuable addition to your toolbox) in the gash, and cut out the hole, following your pencil line. Fasten a pipe or elbow in the plenum hole by *dovetailing* the end—make 3/4″ deep cuts 1 inch apart all around the pipe or elbow; then fold half of the cut tabs out and the remainder inside the plenum, locking the new addition in place.

The pipe is then led to a wall register in your new first-floor room. (One end of each piece of pipe and each fitting is crimped so that it fits inside the mating piece.) For a second-floor room, the pipe must connect with a duct or riser. In many story-and-a-half homes with unfinished attics, thoughtful contractors installed risers inside the walls when the houses were built, saving you a lot of work now. Otherwise, you will have to do the job yourself—and it isn't easy. First, select a location for the riser. Stay away from stud openings with electrical outlets and switches (check this by looking on the first floor, and by noticing in the basement where wires disappear into the floor).

In the basement, carefully measure to locate the floor plate overhead of the partition in which the riser is to be installed. Drill a few 1/2″ holes through the subfloor and the plate to make sure you are in the right place. Then drill pilot holes, and saw out the subfloor and plate to make room for the riser (usually 3-1/4″ × 10″ or 3-1/4″ × 12″).

With a flashlight, carefully inspect the area between the studs above the hole. Make sure that there are no cables or wires crossing the area—if there are, shift the location of the riser. When you are satisfied that the passageway is clear, go to the second floor, and again by careful measuring, find and cut an opening in the top plate to match the one in the basement. Now slide the riser down (or up) through the holes, hook up the piping in the basement, and use duct or pipe as necessary to lead from the riser to a floor or wall register.

You may be able to save yourself all that work if you have a strategically located closet or utility room on the first floor through which you can lead the riser without having to run it up through a wall. You may also find it preferable to locate it in a corner of some room and box it in, or make it a part of a built-in bookshelf or cabinet.

A gravity system is not usually effective for heating a basement since it operates on the principle of heat rising, while you want the heat to go down in a basement room.

With a forced-circulation system, on the other hand, there are several possibilities for basement heating. If the ductwork passes through the area to be heated, you can install a register or registers by cutting into the bottom or side of the duct (as through the plenum of a gravity furnace, above). If the duct is to be boxed in, have short collars made at a sheet metal shop to bring the registers level with the surface of the new ceiling.

If ductwork does not pass through the basement area to be heated, or if it is off to one side, a new heat run can be tapped into the side or top of the duct (just like tapping into the gravity plenum, above) and pipe (4″ to 6″) run between joists to a ceiling register, or down through a partition to a wall outlet. Such ductwork is usually "stepped down" in width as each heat run (the branch lines to individual registers—usually 6″ to 4″ pipe) is "taken off." To add a new run without stepping down (which would require new duct-work), you may have to install a small *baffle* inside the duct to divert the heated air into the run—the baffle is simply a bent piece of metal shaped to catch the air flow; it is held in place with sheet metal screws.

The same procedure is followed to tap into a duct for a first- or second-floor heat outlet (usually a baseboard diffuser rather than a register). Cutting through and installing a new riser for the second floor is no easier than with gravity heat—the same methods are used.

Where a basement room is adjacent to the furnace, you can

tap directly into the plenum of a forced-air unit and run a short duct (easily made to your specifications by a sheet metal shop) to a register cut into the separating partition. You can also cut into the plenum to run pipe to an upstairs heat outlet. As above, a baffle may be needed, especially if a main duct line runs off the same side of the plenum.

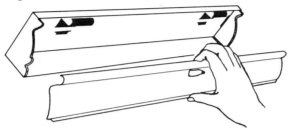

Figure 9-6: If the capacity of your present hot air furnace is adequate, a baseboard diffuser like this can be used to heat your new room.

A forced-air furnace depends on the circulation of air. If you expect to increase its output of heated air by adding new outlets, you must also increase its air intake by increasing the number of cold air returns. In the basement, this is relatively easy; just put a grille at floor level and pipe it to the cold air drop or plenum on the furnace—the part that feeds air to the blower compartment. It's also easy to cut a return opening into the wall or floor of a first floor room and duct or pipe it to the return drop. It is considerably more difficult to do this in a second-floor room. The easy solution is to cut a return somewhere near the foot of the stairs on the first floor, to draw the cold air from upstairs and direct it to the furnace. While this may mean a somewhat drafty staircase, it is a compromise that generally works.

IF THE OLD FURNACE WON'T DO . . .

Suppose, by your own calculations and on the advice of the experts, you realize that your present furnace doesn't have the capacity to heat your newfound space. You have a number of options.

You may decide that it's time to chuck the old unit and install a modern, efficient, and larger furnace that can take care of all your heating needs—including the new room. This might be an especially wise choice if you are still stoking an ancient gravity model with an enormous fuel appetite. At this stage, you might even opt for a completely new ductwork system that will give you considerably more basement headroom in addition to the space you will gain by

Figure 9-7: If the present furnace is already working at full load, one solution is to install a second, small unit to heat the new space. Here, a hot air furnace is located in the corner closet of a family room. Outside the closet, an air conditioner utilizes the same ductwork.

having a compact modern furnace to replace the old behemoth. This will also allow cheap and easy central air conditioning. (See page 156.)

Or maybe the old (or not so old) furnace is doing a good job, keeping your family cozy without emptying your wallet every other week during the winter. But the geography is all wrong—that is, the furnace is located at one end of the basement while the new room is at the other end, and it seems just too much to ask that the piping or ductwork that already runs 40 feet be extended another 12. A

152   solution here is to install another furnace, of small capacity, with its own system of pipes or ductwork to serve the new area exclusively (or even some adjacent rooms to take some of the load off the main furnace). You can often buy used units in perfectly good condition, units that have been replaced by larger capacity furnaces to serve the same purpose that you need to serve. But here a word of warning is in order: Again, ask the experts—your fuel dealer or a representative of the local utility—before investing in a used furnace. It may be perfectly good—or it may be just a piece of trouble.

OTHER NEW-ROOM HEATING SOLUTIONS

Probably the easiest solution to new-room heating problems is the electric baseboard unit. There are several types available, depending on your needs, and most come with specific installation instructions, which should be followed to the letter. Installed along outside walls, they combine warm air with radiant heating and are individually controlled by thermostats.

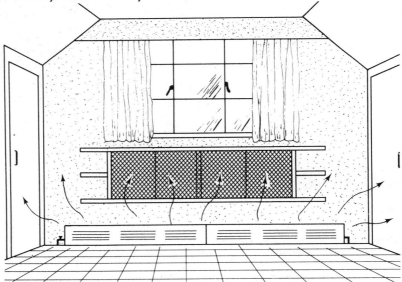

Figure 9-8: Installed on an outer wall, an electric baseboard unit directs a flow of heated air up along the cold wall and throughout the entire room.

Room heaters, both portable and permanent, are available in oil, gas, and electric models. The better ones are automatic and controlled by thermostats. Some models are built into a wall, and some (the gas-fired types) must be vented to the outdoors. Again, follow the manufacturer's recommendations for installation.

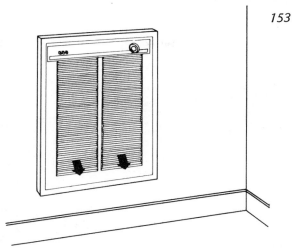

Figure 9-9: The best type of electric wall heater discharges warm air from the bottom and then circulates it by means of a fan. Gas heaters of this type must be vented to the outside.

You are not likely to find a fireplace in an unfinished attic, basement, or garage. But it is not difficult to install either a contemporary prefabricated, freestanding or built-in fireplace as a secondary or even a primary source of heat in a new family room.

Figure 9-10: Freestanding, wood-burning fireplaces are available in a wide range of styles and colors. This one has a prefabricated metal chimney which was cut through the roof of an enclosed porch (*courtesy of Masonite and Condon-King*).

Figure 9-11: Here a freestanding fireplace has been installed in a converted garage (*courtesy of Masonite and Condon-King*).

Figure 9-12: A wall-mounted unit (either gas or electric) will take cool air from a room, warm it and gently force it out at floor level. One like this can be used to heat a large basement (*courtesy of Sears, Roebuck & Company*).

They come in all shapes, sizes, and colors, and in wood-burning and gas-log models. You may be able to vent such a unit through the existing house chimney, or you can install a new prefabricated chimney (but check first with the local building department about

156 their regulations in this regard). Just how the job is done depends on the type of fireplace and chimney you select. Again, be guided by the manufacturer's installation instructions.

Figure 9-13: It looks like a traditional built-in fireplace but the cheery flames come from "gas logs" (no kindling, no messy ashes). And this unit can set against the studding (*right*) or directly on the floor or subfloor (*courtesy of Heatilator Division, Vega Industries*).

AIR CONDITIONING

Summer comfort for your new room poses less of a problem. A room air conditioner can be installed in just about any window—even most basement windows. Or you can install it directly in an outside wall, following normal framing procedures as outlined in Chapter 4. You can even install such a unit in a concrete block wall by removing a few blocks, chiseling adjacent ones away, and then applying asphalt and cementing around the air conditioner. In a concrete wall, the job is, admittedly, a little harder.

If you have central air conditioning, you can cool the new room by cutting into the ductwork—just as for the forced hot-air furnace discussed earlier. In fact, if you have a hot-air system in addition to the central air conditioning, both systems probably utilize the same set of ducts. You will be providing both winter and summer comfort for your new room at the same time.

New Projects for Old Attics

10

An attic remodeling is basically like any other remodeling project with the one big difference noted in earlier chapters—the sloping ceiling walls present problems with headroom. It is the usual practice to erect 4' high *kneewalls* along both sides, using this area for installing beds, desks, or whatever else can be used without standing up. Those with large attics may prefer bringing the walls in to a height of seven or eight feet and eliminating the areas with low headroom, but this leaves larger unused spaces under the eaves.

Even with kneewalls, there will be floor area behind the walls that is a challenge to the imagination of the space-conscious remodeler. One rather expensive and time-consuming, but highly effective, way is to create dormers—or gables, if you will—that raise the effective height all along the length of the dormer. A less extensive but efficient method is to use the behind-the-wall area for storage, sometimes building in shelves, drawers, or other organizers, with or without individual doors.

HOW ONE FAMILY DID IT

The photographs on the next two pages show a remodeling project whereby one family gained 500 extra feet of living space with intelligent planning. The attic was exceptionally small, with an unusual hip roof that made sloping walls on all four sides. If the

158   owners had simply installed kneewalls, they would have had little more space than a large closet.

The first thing they did was to install dormers on three of the four sides. These provided not only added space but also much-needed ventilation and natural light. Since two teen-age boys were to occupy the area, an extra bath was also part of the plan. So that each boy could have a private area if he wished, a drape was installed along a track across the center of the area.

Head space in any attic plan is critical, so the beds were located at the sides of the room, allowing a very comfortable center area for work and play. Note the closed-off shelving and closet in one corner (Figure 10-2), which take full advantage of the difficult eave spaces. To make these shelves, simply lay 3/4″ plywood across the rafters, attaching the backs of the shelves to that and the fronts to your kneewall studs. You can use hardboard between each section, if

Figure 10-1: This hip roof means that the attic has sloping ceilings on all four sides, but intelligent planning utilized the under-eave areas for desks, beds, and built-ins (*courtesy of Azrock Floor Products*).

you desire, or leave the area open. The wardrobe is made the same way, but with a clothes rack in place of the shelves. Doors are made from louvered shutters available in all sizes at most lumber yards, and attached with standard hardware.

Figure 10-2: Close-up views of the new built-in closets and shelves in the attic room (*courtesy of Azrock*).

Another space-minded feature is the perforated hardboard used for storage (Figure 10-3). The desks are simply long tables installed between the built-in shelving along the undormered wall. A complete list of lumber and fixtures may be found on page 162.

Figure 10-3: Perforated hardboard keeps lots of clutter off floors and out of the way. And it is an economical as well as efficient space-saver.

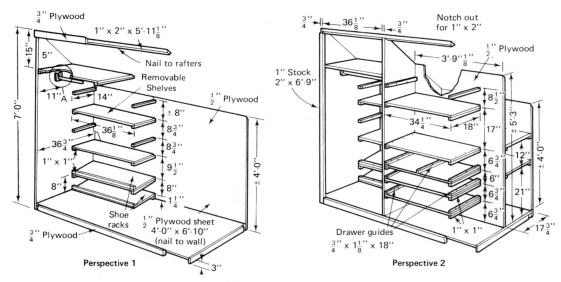

Note: Verify all dimensions to suit individual ceiling slope

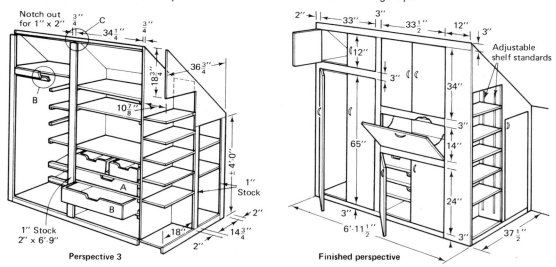

STORAGE UNDER THE EAVES

The plans on these pages show how a compact unit transforms an awkward area into an extremely useful and versatile storage nook. It is easy to build and turns no-headroom areas into useful niches with lots of room for books, knick-knacks, records, or other items. The plan also provides for a built-in desk and wardrobe.

The under-eave storage area shown here is 83-1/2″ long and 37-1/2″ deep, but it can easily be adapted to fit a smaller or larger area if desired. The height and other dimensions are designed for the

CONSTRUCTION DETAILS

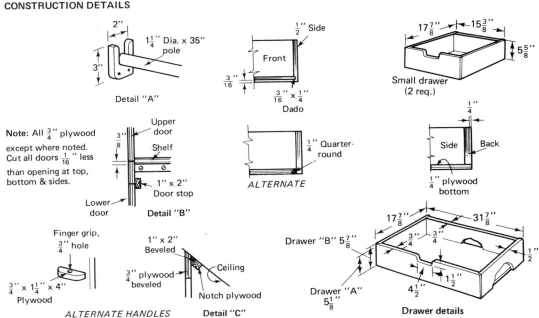

typical rafter angle, but study the plans carefully and check all dimensions for proper fit in your particular situation.

Lay out all plywood parts and cut to size, allowing for saw kerfs. Make sure that the top edges of the sides and partitions are cut to the proper angle to fit the slope of the ceiling, and that the center partition is notched as shown for the beveled 1 x 2-inch frame.

Using 6d finishing nails and glue, apply 3-inch plywood base strips to the bottom. Before installation of the sides and partitions, cut shelf cleats to length and fasten them in position as shown with countersunk screws. Tilt up the bottom so the front edge rests on the floor, and fasten the left side, back, and partition between the wardrobe and drawer space. Apply glue and, with the 1/2" plywood partition in position, nail through the bottom and adjacent partition.

The remaining partition to the right of the drawer space is similarly installed. Be sure to keep the entire assembly in perfect square as the 2 x 2 frame along the top is glued and nailed into place.

After sliding it into position, level the assembly if the floor is uneven (floors usually are). Nail it into place with 8d finishing nails through the 1/2" plywood back into the studs. Install the plywood support for the clothes pole in the wardrobe as shown in detail A, or use standard wood escutcheons if desired. Position and fasten the plywood shelf above; then build shoe racks near the floor as shown.

Materials List 10-1: FOR ATTIC BUILT-INS		
No. or Length	*Description*	*Use*
7	3/4" A-A plywood 4' × 8' (good both sides)	Partitions, door, front, sides, floor, shelves, drawer fronts & backs, desk front
2	1/2" A-D plywood 4' × 8' (good one side)	Interior partition, back, drawer sides
1	1/4" A-D plywood 4' × 4' (good one side)	Drawer bottoms
3'	1-1/4" diameter stock	Clothes pole
12'	1 × 2" stock	Framing, door stop, miscellany
12'	3/4 × 1-1/8" stock	Framing, door stop
44'	1 × 1" stock	Miscellany
12 pairs	Cabinet hinges	Doors
10 each	Friction catches	Doors
10 each	Pulls	Doors
2 each	Metal chains	Drop shelf
18'	Adjustable standards	Shelves
	4d, 6d & 8d finishing nails; glue; flathead screws	As required
	Finishing materials as required	

Cut drawer guides to length, and apply them to the shelves with countersunk screws. Fasten the back shelves in position behind the 1/2" plywood partition. Cut vertical face frames from 1" stock, and apply them with 6d nails and glue. Follow with the installation of a 12" face panel on the right front and triangular-shaped panels over the shelves and the door on the right side.

Dado and rabbet the drawer parts; then assemble and fit them as shown in drawer details. Cut horizontal face frames from 3/4" plywood. Then install them and any needed door stops.

Hang the doors using semi-concealed cabinet hinges. Install friction catches, metal chains for the drop shelf, and door pulls. Ease and sand all edges with No. 1-0 sandpaper. Remove the door pulls, and after filling nailing holes with spackle or wood paste, prepare for finishing by sanding with No. 3-0 sandpaper.

HOW TO INSTALL A SKYLIGHT

Whether you're an artist who likes your subjects viewed under plentiful natural light or just a person who likes rooms flooded with sunshine, a skylight is a great addition to your attic room. It may look like a difficult and complicated job, but it's a lot easier than it appears because this design utilizes existing rafters. With no major framing to be cut, you can do the job in a day or two at most.

First, determine the desired location; then remove the roofing materials from that area. Cut away the roof sheathing, taking care not to cut into the rafters. Nail 1″ boards between the rafters at the top and bottom of the skylight opening to hold insulation in place and to block off these areas.

Nail a 2 x 2 "rib" on top of each rafter (plans on page 164). Measure the width of the Finetex or other wired glass that will be used on the outside of your skylight, and rabbet a piece of 1 x 2 to the width of your glass. Nail the 1 x 2 to the top edge of the 2 x 2 rib, and rabbet the inside. Measure the distance between the top of the sheathing and the top of your rib at the bottom end, and rip a 1″ board to that measurement.

With your sash now complete, place metal flashing over the bottom edge and around the sides. Lay a bed of glazing compound all around each edge, and set the wired glass in place, holding it with metal angle clips screwed to each rib at the bottom and sides of the panel. If you are using more than one pane, make sure that they meet at a rib. Lay another bed of glazing compound at each joint, and put another layer on the top after joining.

After the glass is in place, install the top flashing over the glass and beneath the next row of shingles. See the diagram below. Apply a layer of roofing cement to seal the joint between the flashing and the shingles.

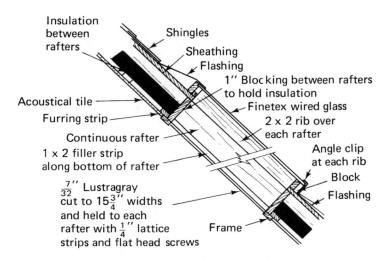

DETAILS OF SKYLIGHT SECTION THROUGH ROOF

The inner glass provides diffused light and an insulation space. Use American St. Gobain Lustragray or similar glass 7/32" thick. Cut individual panels between each rafter. Standard 16" o.c. rafters will take panels 15-3/4" wide.

Nail 1 x 2 furring strips below each rafter to level them with the furring for the ceiling tile, or use whatever method is appropriate to make the bottom of the glass level with the bottom edge of your ceiling material. Each panel is secured to the rafter furring with 1/4" lattice strips screwed into the rafters.

BUILD AN ALCOVE BED

Clever decorating can make difficult alcove beds look just as pretty as any of those in downstairs rooms. The one shown in Figure 10-4 looks like something special, mainly because of the matching valance and drapes. The light blue easy-maintenance Marlite walls are run to the ceiling and match the decor in the study room. Other nice touches are the woodgrain paneling, oval mirror, and mood-setting pictures along the wall. If you can produce a similar effect in your attic, your children will all be fighting to sleep there.

Figure 10-4: A little imagination and some careful work transformed an awkward attic corner into an attractive sleeping alcove for a schoolgirl installed in her own private quarters (*courtesy of Marlite Paneling*).

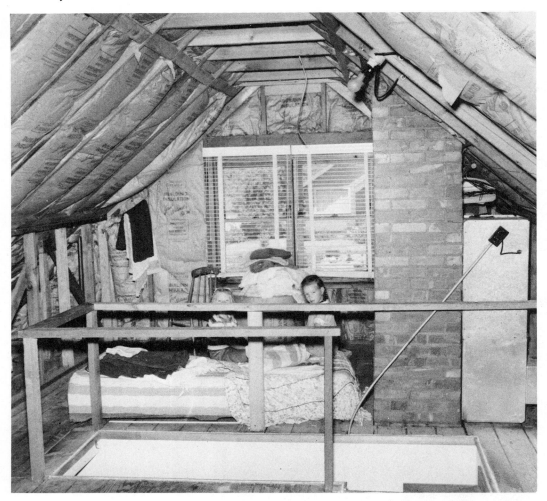

Figure 10-5: This unfinished, dangerous, and cramped attic space underwent a radical change (see the facing page).

BE A SPACE TIGHTWAD

With living space in a home valued at $20 and more per square foot, it is vital that your remodeling project not waste a single inch. We have discussed using the under-eave areas for storage, plus several other space-saving designs. The *before* and *after* photographs above dramatically illustrate the virtue of planned space miserliness.

Note in the *before* picture that the children had to contend not only with an ugly attic area for a bedroom but also with very cramped conditions and a downright hazard to life and limb with their bed so near the unprotected stairwell.

Figure 10-6: One of the many excellent borrowable ideas is the use here of trundle beds under the eaves of this "new-found" play area and bedroom (*courtesy of American Plywood Association*).

The old chimney, a useless relic from the days of the wood stove, was removed. The stairwell was relocated and provided with adequate railings. Still, the extra space would have been much smaller, had not the beds been trundled under the eaves. Now, the children have adequate sleeping room at night, but the beds can be pushed completely out of the way during the day for plenty of play room.

167

The beds shown here were made to order, but many bunk beds come with trundling hardware supplied, and they can be adapted to under-eave areas like those shown. Attachments for making trundle beds are available at bedding and hardware stores.

Also note the efficient use of the end of the attic with built-in plywood shelves, drawers, and play areas. The desk-play areas are built so that the stools can be pushed underneath when not in use. Plywood, 3/8″ thick, is also used to cover the rafters.

COMBINATION BED AND CEDAR CHEST

Another way of utilizing scarce living space is to make things do double duty. If you're ingenious (and lucky) enough, you may manage a triple threat like the storage sofa-bed on these pages. This unit can be set into a low-ceilinged area, providing comfortable seating as well as doubling as an extra bed when the back is removed. Not only that, it also triples as a spacious storage area. The complete unit can be built for about $100.

Construction of a sofa–bed–chest is relatively simple. On a frame of 2 x 4s attach a standard 3′0″ x 6′8″ hollow-core door. The door, forming the bottom of the bed and the top of the chest, is flush at the back and has a 6″ overhang at the front and ends.

Nailed to the 2 x 4 chest framing are 3-1/2″ wide pieces of tongue-and-groove aromatic red cedar. The cedar lining on the inside of the chest is left in its natural state for moth-repellency; the outside is sealed and varnished.

Figure 10-7: This ingenious combination sofa bed-storage unit is ideal for small attic rooms.

A drop-down hinged door consists of the same cedar lining material glued and tacked to both sides of a 1/2" piece of hardboard. A setback along the four edges of the door permits the door to close tightly and retain the cedar fragrance.

A section of chain at each end of the door lets the door open a maximum of 180 degrees, stopping it an inch or two off the floor and providing an access platform for transferring articles in and out of the storage chest.

A 4" thick piece of foam rubber padding covered with green felt (any heavy fabric can be used) forms the seat cushion. Back cushions also are made of upholstered foam rubber.

The bolsters rest up against two removable, rectangular storage compartments that are built on a light wood frame covered with 1/4" hardboard and upholstered to match the bolsters and seat cushion. The compartments act as spacers to narrow the width of the bed when it's used as a sofa and, with openings in the back, to provide storage for pillows and bedding.

Figure 10-8: Opened up, the sofa bed reveals a small "cedar chest." Construction details are diagrammed on the next page.

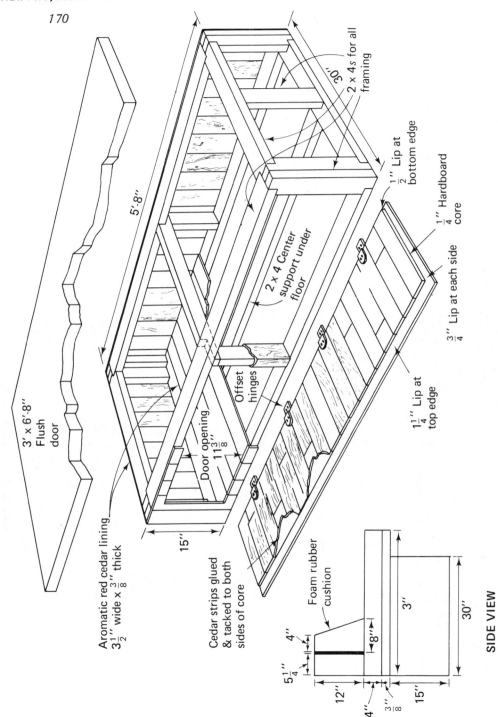

3' x 6'-8" Flush door

5'-8"

30"

2 x 4s for all framing

$\frac{1}{2}$" Lip at bottom edge

$\frac{1}{4}$" Hardboard core

$\frac{3}{4}$" Lip at each side

2 x 4 Center support under floor

$1\frac{1}{4}$" Lip at top edge

Offset hinges

Door opening $11\frac{3}{8}$"

15"

Aromatic red cedar lining $3\frac{1}{2}$" wide x $\frac{3}{8}$" thick

Cedar strips glued & tacked to both sides of core

Foam rubber cushion

4"

$5\frac{1}{4}$"

8"

3"

30"

12"

4"

$\frac{3}{8}$"

15"

SIDE VIEW

Figure 10-9: Cut and fit all materials exactly as laid out here for the storage unit-sofa bed illustrated on pages 168 and 169.

Ideas for the "Rec" Room

11

Basement Recreation Rooms

It is commonly supposed that the "rec" in rec room is short for recreation, but some critics contend that it should be "wreck," particularly if inhabited by kids or teen-agers. Either . way, it illustrates an important consideration—the room should be built not only for fun, but also to withstand a certain amount of punishment.

In most cases, the recreation room is in the basement, although it can be built elsewhere, too. An attic is probably a poor place because of the noise, but a garage or another room away from the main living area is all right. If you have a choice, however, opt for the basement. The projects in this chapter assume that the recreation room is located in the basement. If built elsewhere, simply make the appropriate adjustments.

THEME: "SAILOR'S HAVEN"

A nautical theme is a natural for basements, and the one shown next is exceptionally well executed. Fidelity to the design gives it esthetic unity and careful planning makes it work. Study the floor plan and elevations on pages 173-75.

The room contains many decorative pieces reminiscent of the sea. The most eye-catching accessory and the center of interest is the handsome figurehead with her sea-weathered coloring. This particularly fine reproduction was secured from Jo Mead Designs in

Figure 11-1: Skillful execution of a plan with a theme makes this recreation room a recreation haven.

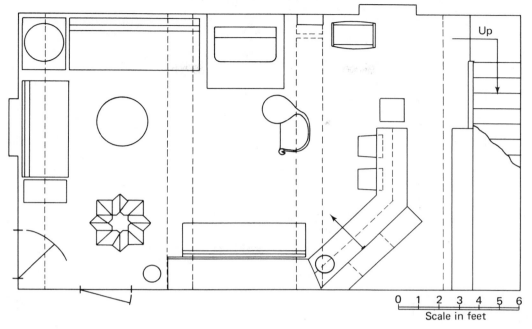

Figure 11-2: Floor plan for "Sailor's Haven" shown on page 172. Details are re-produced below and on the following pages.

Chicago. Not quite as impressive—but less expensive—are other nautical decorations such as ships' lanterns, driftwood, sea grasses, coral, old anchors, shells, and many other items from the briny deep.

Another inexpensive nautical feature is the compass rose inset, which can be cut from floor tile with a pair of scissors. The pattern is given on page 174.

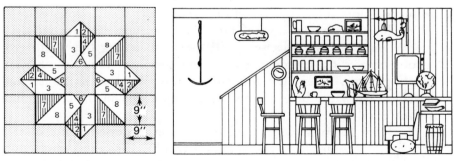

Figure 11-3: Details for making the "compass rose" out of floor tiles are shown on page 174.

COMPASS ROSE INSET

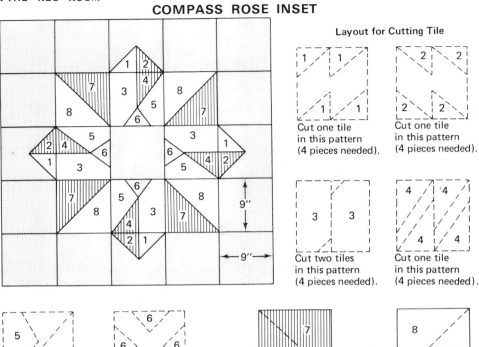

Layout for Cutting Tile

Cut one tile in this pattern (4 pieces needed).

Cut one tile in this pattern (4 pieces needed).

Cut two tiles in this pattern (4 pieces needed).

Cut one tile in this pattern (4 pieces needed).

Cut two tiles in this pattern (4 pieces needed).

Cut one tile in this pattern (4 pieces needed).

Be sure to cut two diagonals as shown in each color so that pattern stays the same for all corners. (Nos. 7 and 8)

Figure 11-4: Layout and cutting diagrams for the compass rose made from floor tiles. A minimum of 25 resilient tiles should be set aside. Colors should be selected to suit the nautical theme.

Not so evident in our black-and-white photograph are the seascape colors—blues, grays, white, sandy beiges, and sunny golds—all made more dramatic with stark black accents. The tongue-and-groove paneling is a silver-gray driftwood matching the weathered wood shingles of seaside cottages, and the floor tile, although an older pattern, resembles the fine white pebbles of Nantucket beaches. The clear blue of the sky is duplicated in the ceiling and staircase walls.

This room is well suited to the construction talents of the average do-it-yourselfer. The walls are real brick painted white, but could be made just as effectively with one of the many fine imitation bricks available today, and you don't have to paint them—most come in white. Or simply paint the concrete with white masonry paint.

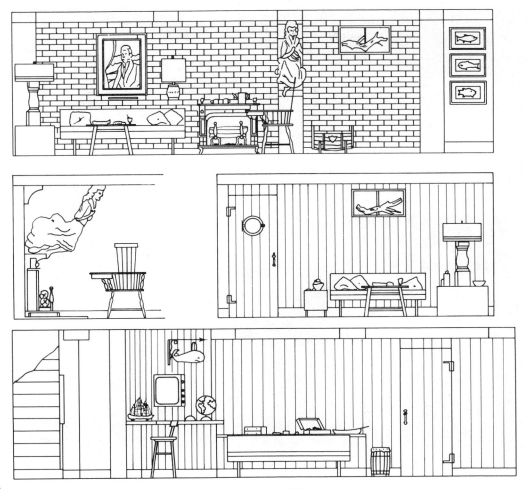

Figure 11-5: These elevations and the one on page 173 show exactly how to lay out the four walls of this recreation room.

The beams are built up with wood blocks and finishing boards, or you can buy prefabricated rustic wood or artificial beams.

The bar stools are modeled after captain's chairs. They have some modern touches, though, with plastic cushions and swiveled bases. The unique Windsor chair has an extremely high back and a most useful appendage—a built-on arm table complete with drawer.

The bar counter and the wall behind it angle at the corner of the room and then return along the adjoining longer wall, ending with a built-in stereo. The three small sofas are perfect for lounging and watching the built-in TV behind the bar.

Figure 11-6: A "recycled" basement becomes a recreation area with some of the fun and convenience of a sidewalk café (*courtesy of Masonite Corporation*).

"GAY PAREE" ROOM

You can bring the charm and the color of "gay Paree" into your recreation room by adapting the continental atmosphere of this plan to suit your own decorating scheme. Most of the easy-to-follow construction details are shown, and they can be used as is or altered to your needs. Check the appropriate chapters of this book for instructions as to dampness control, framing, heating, wiring, etc.

Some of the particulars that should be mentioned are the permanently closed shutters and the planter box. The shutters under the window give it a larger appearance and tend to draw it down from the top of the wall. Small, high basement windows are rather ugly unless given some treatment such as this.

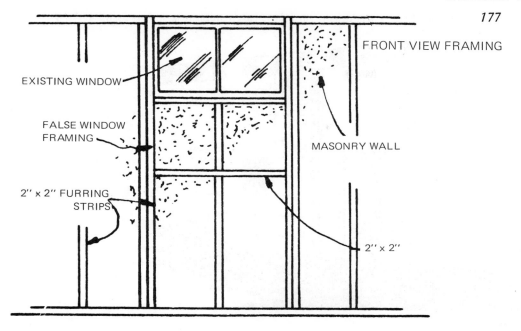

FRONT VIEW FRAMING

EXISTING WINDOW

FALSE WINDOW
FRAMING

MASONRY WALL

2" x 2" FURRING
STRIPS

2" x 2"

FINISHED WINDOW TREATMENT

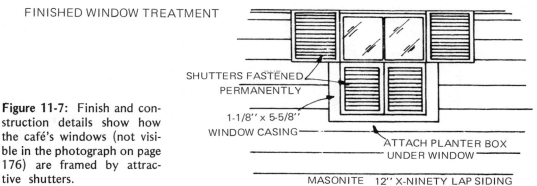

SHUTTERS FASTENED
PERMANENTLY

1-1/8" x 5-5/8"
WINDOW CASING

ATTACH PLANTER BOX
UNDER WINDOW

MASONITE   12" X-NINETY LAP SIDING

Figure 11-7: Finish and construction details show how the café's windows (not visible in the photograph on page 176) are framed by attractive shutters.

The planter box is fastened to the wall with metal brackets. These, plus the wrought iron standards at the pole and the end of the bar, should be available at your building supply dealer. If not, there are wrought iron companies in most areas that will have them.

The tempered hardboard used in the shutters and in other places should be conditioned first in your basement before application. Instructions are given in the application sheets available from your supplier. The hardboard and the X-90 siding used for the "outside" walls are finished like ordinary wood. The X-90 siding comes already primed. The Presdwood hardboard needs a good primer and a compatible finish.

178 **Figure 11-8:** This drawing shows the cafe's stationary and swinging shutters.

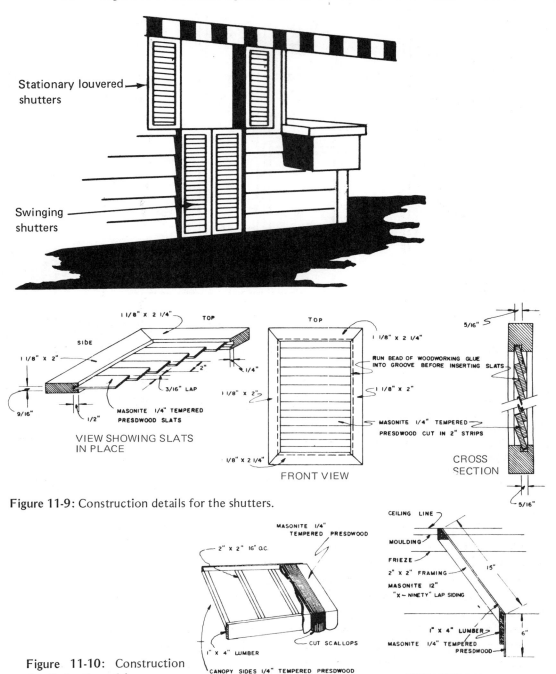

Stationary louvered shutters

Swinging shutters

Figure 11-9: Construction details for the shutters.

VIEW SHOWING SLATS IN PLACE

FRONT VIEW

CROSS SECTION

Figure 11-10: Construction details for the cafe's canopy.

SIDE VIEW CANOPY

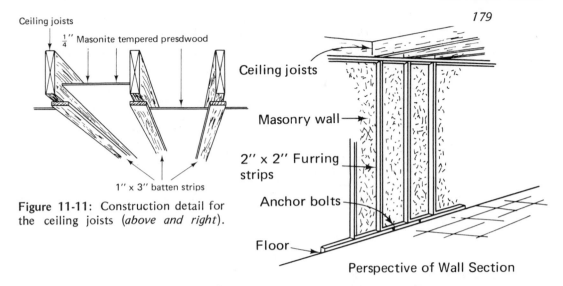

Ceiling joists

$\frac{1}{4}$" Masonite tempered presdwood

1" x 3" batten strips

Figure 11-11: Construction detail for the ceiling joists (*above and right*).

Ceiling joists

Masonry wall

2" x 2" Furring strips

Anchor bolts

Floor

Perspective of Wall Section

Figure 11-12: This perspective view shows the general layout for the wall sections of the café.

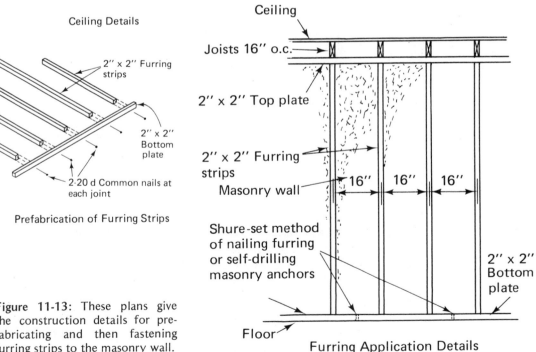

Ceiling Details

2" x 2" Furring strips

2" x 2" Bottom plate

2-20 d Common nails at each joint

Prefabrication of Furring Strips

Figure 11-13: These plans give the construction details for prefabricating and then fastening furring strips to the masonry wall.

Ceiling

Joists 16" o.c.

2" x 2" Top plate

2" x 2" Furring strips

Masonry wall

16"   16"   16"

Shure-set method of nailing furring or self-drilling masonry anchors

2" x 2" Bottom plate

Floor

Furring Application Details

To determine the number of siding courses needed for your Gay Paree room, measure the distance from the ceiling to the floor at its lowest point. Divide this figure by 10-1/2 or 11, depending on the amount of lap desired. Any remainder will be taken up by your starter strip.

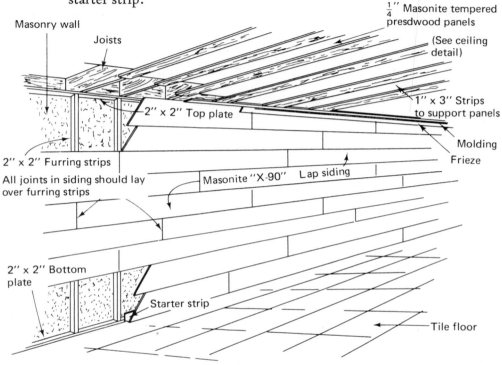

Masonry wall

Joists

$\frac{1}{4}''$ Masonite tempered presdwood panels

(See ceiling detail)

2" x 2" Top plate

1" x 3" Strips to support panels

Molding

Frieze

2" x 2" Furring strips

All joints in siding should lay over furring strips

Masonite "X-90" Lap siding

2" x 2" Bottom plate

Starter strip

Tile floor

APPLICATION OF SIDING AND CEILING DETAIL

Figure 11-14: Application of the lap siding begins with the starter strip at the foot of the wall. The X-90 siding is fastened to the furring strips with 8d siding nails.

The starter strip should be placed firmly against the wall in the position it will occupy. Scribe a line along the length of the strip with a compass, following the contour of the floor. Then cut along the scribed line with a fine-toothed handsaw or power saw with a combination blade. The siding is attached to the furring with 8d siding nails. Drive the nails in at least 1/2" from the bottom edges and ends. Follow the guidelines on the face of the siding to maintain level courses. Use 1-1/8" square lumber for inside corners, and special metal corners (available at your dealer) for outside edges.

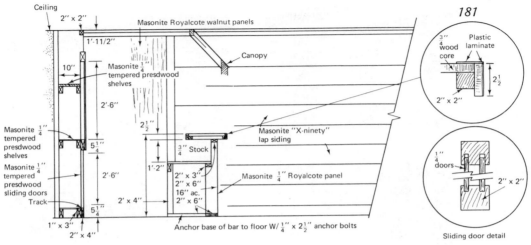

Ceiling

2" x 2"

Masonite Royalcote walnut panels

1'-11/2"

Canopy

10"

Masonite $\frac{1}{4}$" tempered presdwood shelves

$\frac{3}{4}$" wood core

Plastic laminate

2" x 2"

$2\frac{1}{2}$

2'-6"

$2\frac{1}{2}$

$\frac{3}{4}$" Stock

Masonite "X-ninety" lap siding

Masonite $\frac{1}{4}$" tempered presdwood shelves

$5\frac{1}{4}$"

$\frac{1}{4}$" doors

2" x 2"

Masonite $\frac{1}{4}$" tempered presdwood sliding doors

2'-6"

1'-2"

2" x 3"
2" x 6"
16" ac.
2" x 6"

Masonite $\frac{1}{4}$" Royalcote panel

Track

$5\frac{1}{4}$"

2' x 4"

1" x 3"

2" x 4"

Anchor base of bar to floor W/ $\frac{1}{4}$" x $2\frac{1}{2}$" anchor bolts

Sliding door detail

Figure 11-15: Section bar area (*above*) and bar top detail (*right*).

Plastic laminate $\frac{3}{4}$" stock

2" x 2" 12" o.c.

2" x 2" Furring strips

3'5"

1'5"

2" x 2" Furring strips

Masonite $\frac{1}{4}$" Royalcote walnut panels

Masonite "X-ninety" lap siding

Louvered shutter doors

3'-0"

7'-2"

Masonite $\frac{1}{4}$" tempered presdwood lining in storage area

1'-5$\frac{1}{2}$"

10" 16"

Figure 11-16: Plan view of bar area (*right*). All plans shown on pages 177-81 and a description of the necessary materials may be obtained as Plan AE-401 from the Masonite Corporation.

2" x 6"

2" x 4"

Louvered shutter doors

1'-2" 2'-0" 1'-3" 2'-2"

Figure 11-17: This recreation room is an excellent example of a unifying theme—here a Western motif (*courtesy of Armstrong Cork*).

SETTING A DECORATIVE THEME

There's nothing wrong, of course, with a recreation room that's just plain comfortable and fun to be in. But the looks and effectiveness of your recreation room are greatly enhanced if you follow a unifying theme, like the outdoor cafe look in our "Gay Paree" room or the nautical atmosphere in the "Sailor's Haven."

The photographs on pages 182-186 also show how recreation rooms can be given a special appearance by unifying the materials and decor around a family interest such as the Old West, baseball, card playing, etc. The four photographs on pages 186-187 demonstrate how unusual materials such as canvas can be used to create a circus atmosphere.

Figure 11-18: Workroom of the late Cornelius Ryan, author-historian, shows his passionate interest in World War II. Note the battle maps on the wall under the clocks and the abundant shelving for his reference books (*courtesy of Karastan Rugs*).

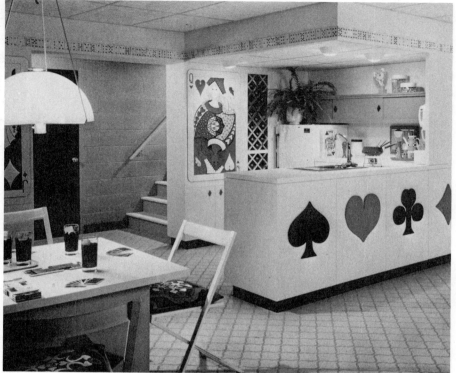

Figure 11-19: A family's interest in contract bridge provides the decorative theme for a handsome party room (*courtesy of Armstrong Cork*).

THE BAR: COCKTAIL, DAIRY, OR SODA

Even if you don't drink, a bar may be an essential part of your recreation planning. Surely some of your guests will be drinkers, and, if not, you should build a dairy or soda-pop bar for the kids. A bar is a naturally friendly place for convivial convening.

The bar can be unobtrusively tucked away in a corner, or it can be the focal point of your family room. It can be a permanent fixture, a portable unit on casters, or a fold-away. Plain, simple or elaborate, a bar can set the decorative tone for the whole room.

Normal bar height is 42 inches, but you can size yours to suit yourself—make it table height (30 inches) if you prefer to sit on chairs rather than stools. The bar top should be of a tough material. Plastic laminate makes a good modern-day substitute for the traditional mahogany. (If you prefer wood, though, be sure to give the bar top several coats of hard plastic varnish.) And don't forget to provide shelf space for bottles, glassware, and bar supplies.

Figure 11-20: Special interests provided ideas here, too: a room for a passionate volunteer fireman (*above*) and one for a devotee of Early American (*below*).

Figure 11-21: This recreation area's styling reflects the owner's interest in English Tudor (*courtesy of Masonite Corporation*).

Figure 11-22: An all too typical "before" basement was actually neater than many, but not particularly attractive.

Figure 11-23: "After" shows the careful work an enterprising do-it-yourselfer accomplished with canvas, compression poles and twine.

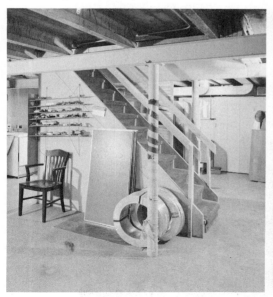

Figure 11-24: Bright, different and inexpensive to make, this Circus Room demonstrates enjoyable creativity (*courtesy of Canvas Awning Institute*).

Glass Bar

A hospitable invitation to relax is exuded along with the softly diffused light that makes this bar a favorite with guests and host alike. The sophisticated elegance of the backlighted patterned glass of both the bar and the wall cabinet behind is at home in any surroundings. Visit a glass supplier to see the many varieties of patterned glass available.

Figure 11-25: Sketch of "Glass Bar" only hints at its eye-catching appeal.

To build the bar, cut four 3/4″ plywood uprights (see Materials List 11-1). Screw 1×4 cleats where shown to the insides of the end uprights and to both sides of the intermediate uprights. Assemble the uprights in place with the 1×6 front kickboard and footrail, and the 1×6 rear spacers. Anchor the assembly to the floor with metal angles fastened to the floor and the insides of the end uprights. Then fasten the lower shelf pieces to the cleats.

Glue and screw the 3/4" plywood top to 1 x 2 cleats fastened
to the uprights, or secure the top to the uprights with small metal
angles screwed to both members. The bar top is then covered with a
wood-grain plastic laminate, with metal edge molding.

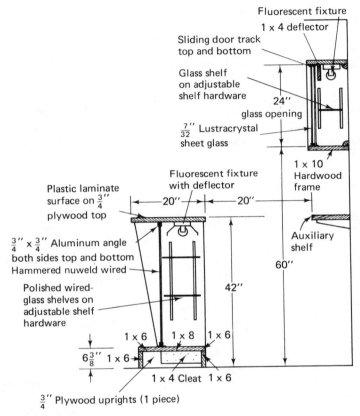

Figure 11-26: Layout shows how glass, plywood, and hardware are used for an elegant home bar.

Screw aluminum angles at the top and bottom to provide
backing for the patterned glass face pieces. Cushion the edges of the
glass with plastic tape; then set in place. Secure it with an aluminum
angle in front of the glass.

Install standard fluorescent fixtures with metal deflectors on
the underside of the bar top. Then attach adjustable shelf brackets to
the uprights to support the glass shelves.

For the backbar cabinet, build a rectangular frame of 1 x 10
hardwood, and mount it on cleats that are firmly secured to all studs.

Materials List 11-1: FOR GLASS BAR

No. or Length	Description	Use
1	3/4" × 4' × 8' INT A-A plywood	Uprights
1	3/4" × 20" × 8' INT A-D plywood	Bar top
1	1" × 4" × 6' lumber	Cleats
4	1" × 6" × 8' lumber	Kickboard, footrail, shelves
1	1" × 8" × 8' lumber	Shelves
1	30" × 8' plastic laminate	Bar, shelf top
20'	Edge molding	Bar, shelf edging
12'	Metal angles	Bottom, top fastening
32'	Aluminum angle	Glass front
3	31 × 34-3/4" patterned glass	Front
12	2' shelf standards with brackets	Shelves
6	12 × 30-1/2" glass shelves	Under bar
5	1" × 10" × 8' lumber	Cabinet, shelf
1	1" × 10" × 4' lumber	Cabinet, sides
2	1" × 2" × 1' lumber	Wall cleats
1	1" × 4" × 8' lumber	Deflector
2	8' door tracks	Sliding doors
2	23" × 4' patterned glass	Cabinet doors
4	Shelf brackets	Auxiliary shelf
	Fluorescent fixtures, cabinet shelving, & hardware	As required

Install a fluorescent fixture at the top, and fasten a 1 x 4 deflector board in front of the fixture. Affix the sliding door track at the top and bottom. Fit the doors of sheet glass into the tracks. Install the partitions and shelves as desired.

Exposed wood parts of the bar and cabinet are primed and painted to suit the room decor. An auxiliary shelf of 1 x 10 lumber covered with plastic laminate is fastened to the wall with shelf cleats as a final touch.

Built-In Swinging Bar

If your space is limited, you may prefer to have a bar that is out of sight when it's out of mind. Behold this swinging built-in!

Figure 11-27: This built-in bar swings out for use—and in for storage.

When it's off duty, it sits quietly in a corner, taking up just 16″ by 4′ of wall space, with never a hint of the goodies it conceals. But when party time rolls around, it rolls out complete with all the ingredients needed to start off an evening of good cheer. Add a few friends, stir with some good conversation, and you can't go wrong. And when the festivities are all over, your bar just folds up and swings silently away, leaving nary a trace.

The unit includes a lighted cabinet in the backbar and a planter on top. Construction is mostly of plywood, with facing of Texture 1-11 grooved paneling.

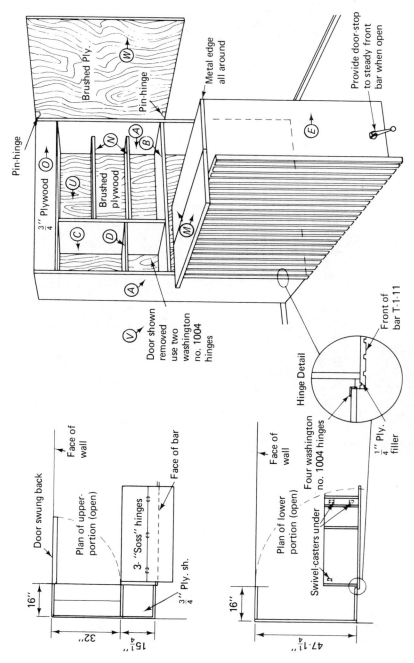

Brushed Ply.

W

Pin-hinge

Pin-hinge

Metal edge
all around

Provide door-stop
to steady front
bar when open

$\frac{3}{4}$" Plywood

O

U

N

A

B

Brushed
plywood

C

D

M

A

E

V

Door shown
removed
use two
washington
no. 1004
hinges

Hinge Detail

Front of
bar T-1-11

$\frac{1}{4}$" Ply.
filler

Face of
wall

Door swung back

Plan of upper-
portion (open)

3- "Soss" hinges

Face of bar

$\frac{3}{4}$" Ply. sh.

16"

32"

15$\frac{1}{4}$"

Face of
wall

Plan of lower
portion (open)

Four washington
no. 1004 hinges

Swivel-casters under

16"

47-11$\frac{1}{4}$"

Figure 11-28: Careful examination of these construction plans and the cutting diagram on page 195 will enable you to do-it-yourself with ease. All necessary materials are also listed on the next pages.

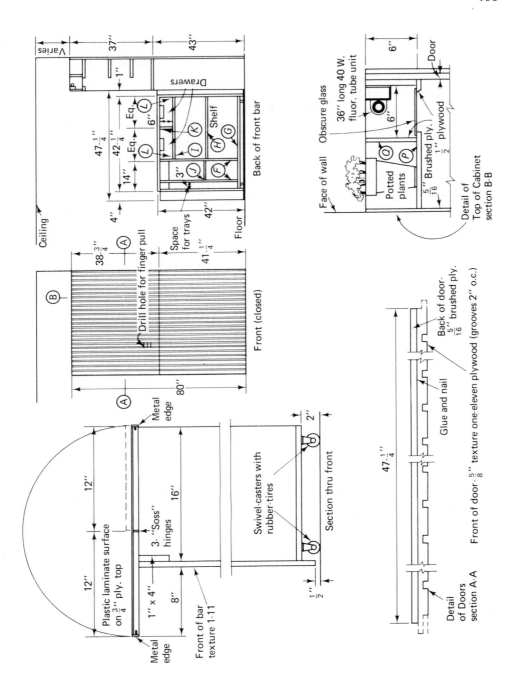

Cut all plywood parts to size, according to the cutting diagrams and the matching key letters in Materials List 11-2. Rabbet sides A 3/8″ deep to receive back panel U. Check it for fit, but do not assemble. With glue and nails, join bottom shelf B, facing strip O, divider Q, light trough bottom P, and partition G to sides A. Be careful to keep the structure square during all these steps; check frequently with a carpenter's square.

Fit and nail back U in place. Nail and glue plywood backs to the Texture 1-11 doors. The intermediate shelves can be nailed in position or installed on adjustable supports after finishing.

Notch bar partitions F and K to allow for 1 x 4 bracing. Because working space is limited, assemble partitions F and K with fixed top M, shelves H, I, J, bottom G, and hinged side E before exposed side E is installed. Install the Texture 1-11 front, hinged top, and casters.

Materials List 11-2: FOR SWINGING BAR

Key	No. or Length	Size of Plywood (INT A-D)	Use
A	2	16 × 80″	Backbar sides
B	1	15-5/8 × 45-3/4″	Backbar lower shelf
C	1	15-5/8 × 30-1/2″	Backbar partition
D	1	14-1/8 × 15-5/8″	Backbar shelf
E	2	15-1/2 × 40-3/4″	Bar sides
F	2	15-1/2 × 38-1/2″	Bar partitions
G	1	15-1/2 × 40-3/4″	Bar bottom shelf
H	1	15-1/2 × 26-3/4″	Bar shelf
I	1	15-1/2 × 26-3/4″	Drawer shelf
J	1	9-1/2 × 15-1/2″	Bar shelf
K	1	6 × 15-1/2″	Divider
L	2	6 × 13″	Drawer front
M	2	12 × 42-1/4″	Bar top
N	2	8 × 30-7/8″	Backbar shelves
O	1	6 × 45-3/4″	Light trough face
P	1	15-5/8 × 45-3/4″	Planter box bottom
Q	1	6 × 45-3/4″	Top divider
R	4	5-7/8 × 14-3/8″	Drawer sides
S	2	5-7/8 × 12″	Drawer backs
T	2	12 × 13-7/8″	Drawer bottoms
U	1	46-1/2 × 80″	Backbar back
V	1	16 × 38-3/4″	Door backing
W	1	31-1/4 × 38-3/4″	Door backing
		Texture 1-11 doors	
		& bar front cut	
		to fit backing pieces	

Materials List 11-2: *(continued)*

No. or Length	Description of Miscellany	Use
1	1/4 × 1 × 42″ wood	Fillers
1	1 × 4 × 42″ lumber	Bracing
1	36″ 40W fluorescent fixture	Cabinet
1	5-1/2 × 45-3/8″ obscure glass	Cabinet top
2	12 × 42-1/2″ plastic laminate	Top
1	3/4″ × 11-1/2′ metal edging	Bar edge
3	Concealed hinges	Bar top
6	3/4″ hinges	Bar door
2	Pin hinges	Large door
3	Rubber-wheel casters	Bar
1	Door stop	Bar

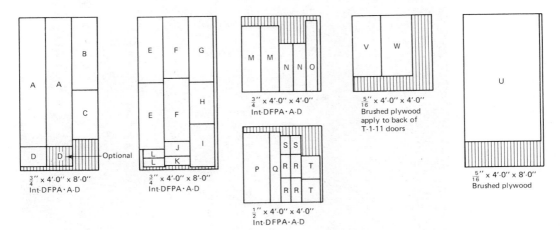

Figure 11-29: Cutting diagram for plywood pieces used to make the Swinging Bar.

Finish the unit with either oil- or water-base paint. When water-base paint is used, seal the plywood first with clear resin sealer or oil-base primer. After priming, apply two coats of compatible paint or enamel, allowing adequate drying time between coats as recommended by the manufacturer.

Move the backbar into position against the wall after the final finishing. Lastly, attach the doors and the hinged front bar.

Other Bar Ideas

You may prefer, of course, to construct your own personally designed bar from scratch. Space limitations and other needs dictate the size and type of bar you may want to build, but perhaps you can find ideas to adapt in the three projects illustrated next.

Figure 11-30: Shakertown shingle panels make an interesting rustic wall.

A SHINGLE WALL INDOORS

There are all kinds of decorating ideas, of course, and we saw how outside siding can be used indoors for the "Gay Paree" room. Another use of outdoor materials inside is the application of cedar shingles to line an accent wall along the back of the basement bar, providing an interesting textured effect.

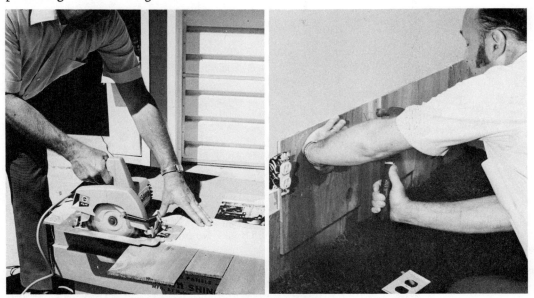

Figure 11-31: The bottom row of shingles is cut along the edge of the backing so that the lower edge is even (*left*). The "cut-offs" are saved for later use on the top panel. The four-foot panels are then nailed into each stud and about four inches down from the top (*right*). Only four nails are required for each panel.

The shingles shown have another unique advantage. Instead of having to lay up the shingles one by one, with an increasing chance of error, these red cedar shingles are prealigned in 4' long rows. Even inexperienced do-it-yourselfers can shingle an average wall in a couple of hours. Although they look just like outdoor shingles, the shingles shown are manufactured expressly for indoor use, going under the name of Shakertown Interior-Tex. If not locally available, though, there is no reason why you can't install regular outdoor shakes.

To install the shingle panels, simply nail them to the studs or nailing strips. If furring strips are to be installed, it is best to put them up horizontally—on 7-7/8" centers. (Studs should be on 16" centers.) Finishing techniques are shown on the next page.

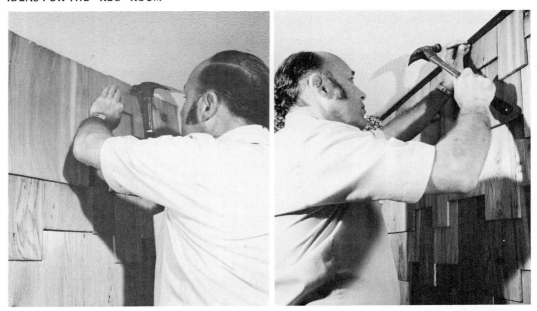

Figure 11-32: The final course is made with the individual shingles that were originally cut off from the bottom row. Then the molding is fastened at the top and the job is done—in about two hours. No other finishing is necessary.

Figure 11-33: Don't overlook the possibility of angling the bar when you lay it out for your recreation room.

Figure 11-34: Another interesting project, this one fashioned from plywood; a refrigerator and sink are also included in the party conveniences.

FUN DOWN UNDER

Another essential for the recreation room is some kind of fun. Some of the favorite fun items are table tennis, dart boards, jukeboxes and pinball machines, shuffleboard, TV, game tables, or a plain old "phonograph." Nothing, however—not even the stereo—is as popular as a pool table.

200   Pool tables come in many sizes and types—and in a wide variety of prices. Woe to the homeowner, though, who builds the game room around a pool table and finds that there isn't room for it. This, unfortunately, is not uncommon, mainly because people don't realize how much room is really required.

Figure 11-35: A good pool table is an enjoyable pool table only if it is well lighted and well located in the "rec" room.

The standard basement pool table is 4 x 7 feet, which doesn't seem that much. What people forget is that you need at least three feet all around to wield a pool cue with any comfort. Add three feet to each side, and you get a room—not 4 x 7—but a minimum of 10 x 13. And you may think that a lally pole or two doesn't matter, but it'll surely be in the way for a crucial shot if you plan around it. If you don't have enough room, a bumper pool table is considerably smaller and just as much fun.

AN ENTERTAINMENT COMPLEX

Here's a project that not only is ideal for the basement recreation room, but can also be installed in a family room or elsewhere. The unit shown here was built of Weyerhaeuser cherry plywood, with cherry hardwood doors, but other woods can be used if you prefer.

This entertainment complex is practical and versatile as well as good-looking. It not only houses stereo and radio components, but also has more than adequate storage space for records, tapes, and anything else you feel like tossing into it. Space is provided for a television set, if desired, which can be hidden behind hardwood doors. The entire unit, in fact, can be closed off making it look like a handsome paneled wall. Even with the doors closed, the stereo and radio are not affected since the speakers are above the two side doors.

Figure 11-36: Components, records, and tapes are all accessible in this handsome entertainment complex.

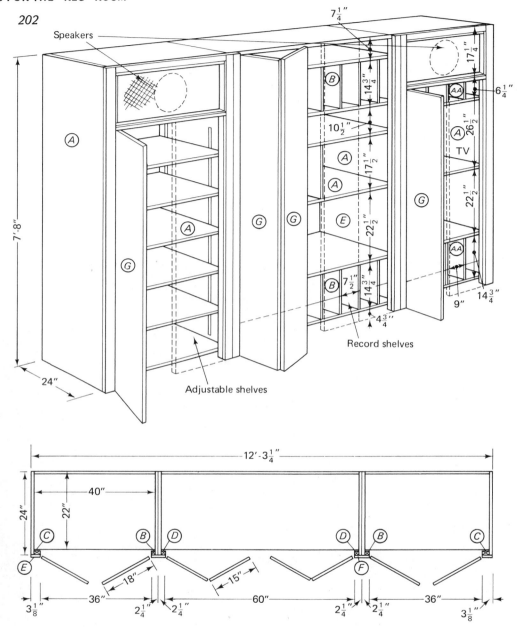

Speakers

$7\frac{1}{4}$"

$17\frac{1}{4}$"

$14\frac{3}{4}$"

$6\frac{1}{4}$"

$10\frac{1}{2}$"

$26\frac{1}{2}$"

TV

$17\frac{1}{2}$"

$22\frac{1}{2}$"

$22\frac{1}{2}$"

$7\frac{1}{2}$" $14\frac{3}{4}$"

$4\frac{3}{4}$"

9" $14\frac{3}{4}$"

Record shelves

7'-8"

24"

Adjustable shelves

12'-$3\frac{1}{4}$"

40"

24"

22"

18"   15"

36" $2\frac{1}{4}$" $2\frac{1}{4}$"   60" $2\frac{1}{4}$" $2\frac{1}{4}$"   36"

$3\frac{1}{8}$" $3\frac{1}{8}$"

You can build just a portion of the complex shown, of course, or alter it to suit your own needs. The dimensions shown are for the average modern home, but you should measure your own area to determine how it will work in your home.

Materials List 11-3: FOR ENTERTAINMENT COMPLEX

Key	No. or Length	Description	Use
LEFT CABINET:			
A	2-1/2 sheets	3/4″ cherry plywood	Shelves and sides
B	11 lin. ft.	2 × 2″ lumber	Framing
C	8 lin. ft.	2 × 3″ lumber	Framing
D	8 lin. ft.	3/4 × 1-1/2″ cherry	Facing
E	11 lin. ft.	3/4 × 3″ cherry	Facing
F	8 lin. ft.	3/4 × 1/4″ cherry	Shelf edges
G	2	1-3/8 × 18 × 72″ cherry doors	Doors
CENTER CABINET:			
A	4-1/2 sheets	3/4″ cherry plywood	Shelves and sides
B	1-1/2 sheets	1/2″ cherry plywood	Dividers
C	21 lin. ft.	2 × 2″ lumber	Framing
D	16 lin. ft.	3/4 × 1-1/2″ cherry	Facing
E	30 lin. ft.	3/4 × 1/4″ cherry	Shelf edges
F	16 lin. ft.	3/4 × 1-1/2″ cherry	Facing
G	4	1-3/8 × 15 × 89″ bifold cherry doors	Doors
RIGHT CABINET:			
A	2 sheets	3/4″ cherry plywood	Shelves and sides
A-A	1/2 sheet	1/2″ cherry plywood	Vertical dividers
B	11 lin. ft.	2 × 2″ lumber	Framing
C	8 lin. ft.	2 × 3″ lumber	Framing
D	8 lin. ft.	3/4 × 1-1/2″ cherry	Facing
E	11 lin. ft.	3/4 × 3″ cherry	Facing
F	8 lin. ft.	3/4 × 1/4″ cherry	Shelf edges
G	2	1-3/8 × 18 × 74″ cherry doors	Doors
HARDWARE FOR EACH DOOR:			
	2	Friction catches	
	2	Sets of knobs	
	2	Pairs of butt hinges	
ADDITIONAL FOR BI-FOLD DOORS:			
	1	5′ folding-door track (top of center cabinet)	
	1	Pair of butt hinges	

Each of the three units shown is built separately and tied together visually with a matching facing board after the sections are set up. The sections are also nailed together through the framing after they are set up.

After you have measured and adapted the complex to your needs and interests, make sure that you make any other changes necessitated by the new dimensions. For small areas, incidentally, you may want to use just the center unit, expanding it and inserting the speakers in the corners.

Start with the framing. If you are building the units into the wall, nail the 2 x 2s and 2 x 3s to the floor and ceiling. If you prefer movable sections, you'll need more framing at the top and bottom. Also, if you are building it in, you won't need the more expensive good-both-sides hardwood on the outside.

After the framing is up, attach the sides with glue and finishing nails. The horizontal shelves are attached next in the same manner. Vertical dividers are then inserted. If you want a really professional job, dado the shelves and dividers before nailing. You can, however, butt these parts if you don't feel up to all that dadoing. Or, if you prefer, use one of the many excellent adjustable shelving systems available at hardware and lumber dealers.

After all the internal members are in place, attach vertical face framing and hang the doors. Standard doors are used in the side cabinets with bi-fold doors in the center cabinet. Most hardwood plywood comes pre-finished, but countersink nails and fill the holes with matching putty.

A Multi-purpose Basement

This section follows a basement remodeling job from start to finish. Very few homeowners will be able to adhere to these plans exactly, and that is not the intent. The room was designed for a specific homeowner, and some plans and photographs are reproduced here to show how the job is actually done. Some of the details can be copied as is, but most will have to be altered to suit your own specifications. The room, however, does contain a lot of good ideas and can provide some construction basics for you to adapt to your own basement.

ONE FAMILY'S NEW BASEMENT

The do-it-yourselfers who remodeled the basement that is illustrated next had several objectives in mind. First, the eight-member family had outgrown its sleeping accommodations, and the two older boys needed to have larger quarters. The family also wanted a sewing room and a workshop. All six children needed more room for studying and reading, and everybody wanted some place to entertain.

A tall order? Yes, especially for a rather small 20×30-foot basement. The area shown here is a compromise, since none of the purposes outlined above could be satisfied completely without eliminating one or more of the others. The result was a genuine multi-purpose living center that is both functional and attractive.

The central or dominant part of the basement is the entertainment/hobby/sewing area which is entered directly from the redesigned staircase. The entertainment section includes a row of wall-mounted cabinets and a built-in storage unit alongside. A long work counter extends the full length under the cabinets.

Slide-away tables, built as part of the project, store under the counter and are used by the children for hobbies and games. They accommodate food and drink when the family is entertaining.

The sewing center occupies the other half of the open area in the finished basement. It features two built-in cabinets, one housing a fold-up cutting table and ironing board and the other storing a portable sewing machine. A three-way mirror along the far wall folds into the wall when the room is being used for entertainment purposes.

The outside walls and sliding doors that open into a newly created bedroom and into the workshop feature Coach House paneling. It is durable hardboard with a look of weathered barn wood. The doors of the cabinets in the entertainment area and sewing center and the tops of the slide-away tables are faced with a plastic-coated tile paneling. The sewing center cabinets are lined with Pegboard panels for handy storage of sewing accessories.

The new bedroom located just off the main room has two built-in coach beds that are all but indestructible. A shuttered window allows ventilation and a choice of sunlight or privacy. Two closets, built on either side of the chimney flue, and two built-in bookcases with adjustable shelves provide ample room for storage of clothes, bedding, and boys' gear.

The new workshop is located in the far corner of the basement. It houses a variety of power and hand tools.

The original staircase was made interesting by turning the bottom two stairs and removing two old treads. A pass-through partition at the foot of the stairs was designed specifically to hide an ugly sewer pipe.

The cushioned-back vinyl flooring used throughout the basement was laid directly over the concrete floor.

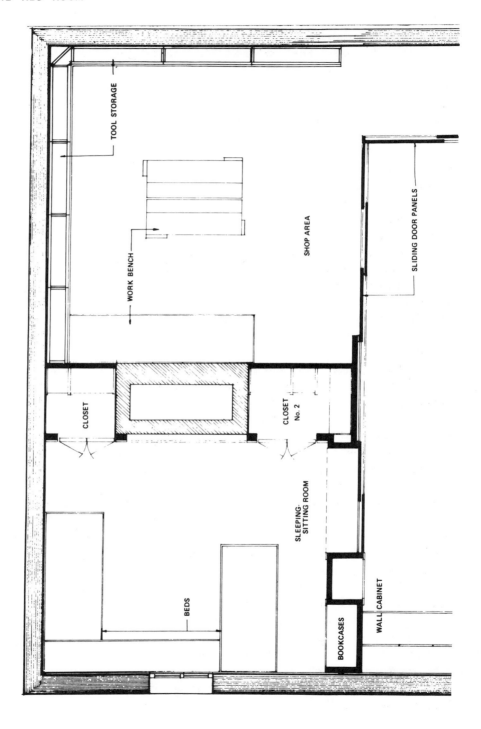

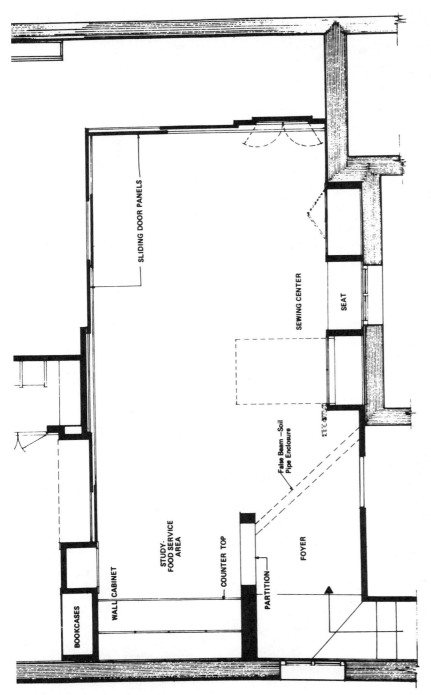

BOOKCASES

WALL CABINET

STUDY-
FOOD SERVICE
AREA

COUNTER TOP

PARTITION

FOYER

False Beam—Soil
Pipe Enclosure

SLIDING DOOR PANELS

SEWING CENTER

SEAT

Figure 11-37: Complete floor plan for the family's new, multi-purpose basement. (*Drawing is not to scale.*)

Figure 11-38: This "before" basement was more miscellaneous than multi-purpose; "after" remodeling it is a functional pleasure—and includes a welcome extra bedroom.

Figure 11-39: View of the main area used by the family for entertainment and hobbies in need of "sound containment." The bedroom pictured on the facing page is actually to the far right of this area; the stairwell is to the left at the rear; and the sewing area shown on the next page is behind the camera from this viewpoint.

Electric heat panels and large fluorescent light grids were set into the ceiling, which consists of pre-finished hardboard paneling with a delicate embossed finish.

Clear pine lumber, stained and varnished, is used as trim on the ceiling and throughout the room and as framing on the sliding doors.

DESIGN YOUR OWN RECREATION AREA

Study the drawings, and incorporate those ideas and features that are suited to your family's needs and tastes. In most cases, 2×3 framing lumber can be used instead of 2×4s, as discussed in previous chapters. Make a similar scale drawing of your own basement area; then compute your materials needs. Before final plans are drawn, check building codes, utility companies, financing agents, etc.

Before starting construction, take whatever steps are necessary to assure dry walls and floor (see Chapter 3). Design hinged

210   doors or push-up ceiling material to allow access to water valves, plumbing clean-outs, or other places you may want to get to later.

Figure 11-40: In this basement there is something for everyone, including a versatile sewing area with recessed machine and cutting table hidden behind bi-fold doors (*above*) and a well-equipped shop (*below*).

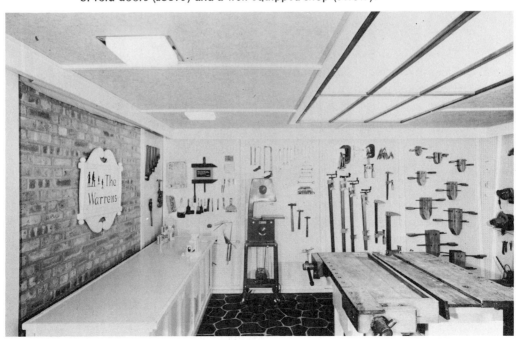

Furring and Framing

Start construction by furring out the foundation walls. Follow the general instructions in Chapter 4 regarding most framing and furring. Specific instructions apply only to the example shown.

Fur the walls at the head of the beds with 2 x 2s to provide better anchoring for beds and shelf. The plan also has space for a standard junction box and convenience outlet on that wall.

Ceiling framing for the fluorescent light grids and heating units is illustrated on page 212. The inside dimensions of the blocking for both light grids are 4-1/4" x 8-1/4". Frame the openings for the light grids with 1 x 3s and 1 x 2s. Use 1 x 3s to block for the electric heat panels so they will be flush with the finished ceiling. The specific pattern and directions to fur out the heating units are included with the units.

The 2 x 2 ceiling panel blocking runs 90 degrees to the joists and 16" on center. Additional headers are required parallel to all panel edges. The blocking lowers the ceiling below electrical junction boxes, wiring, and most water pipes.

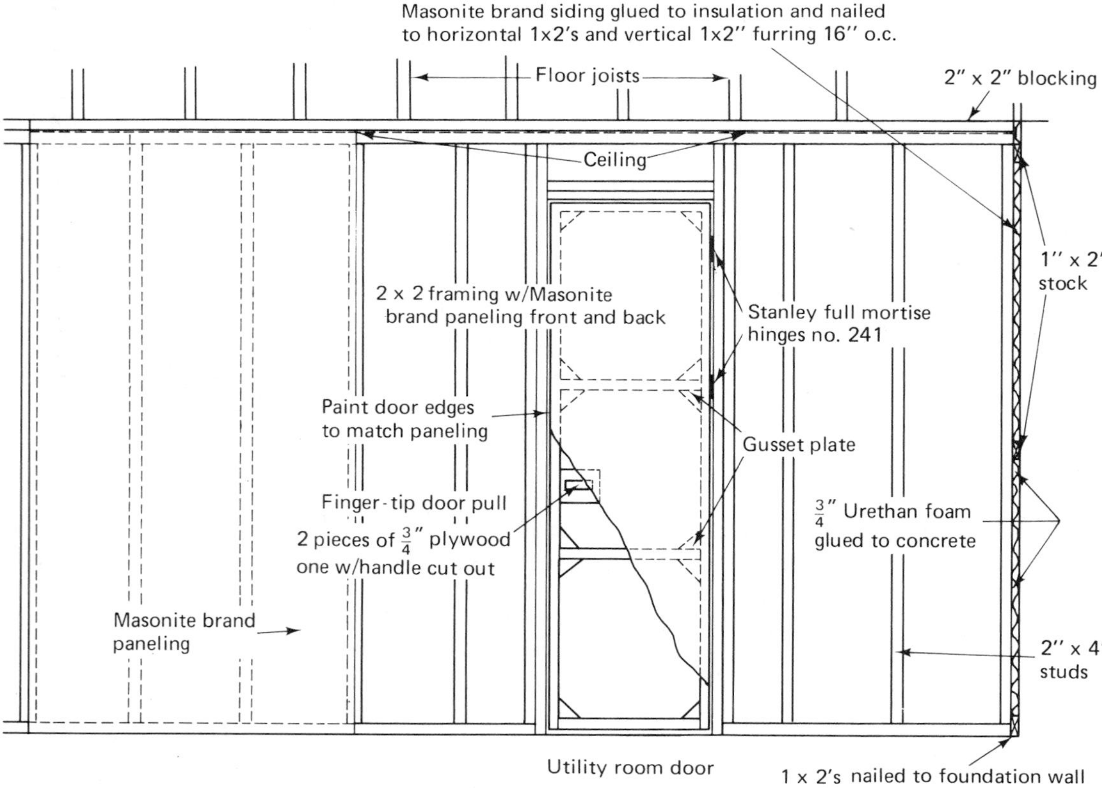

Figure 11-41: Typical framing for interior partitions.

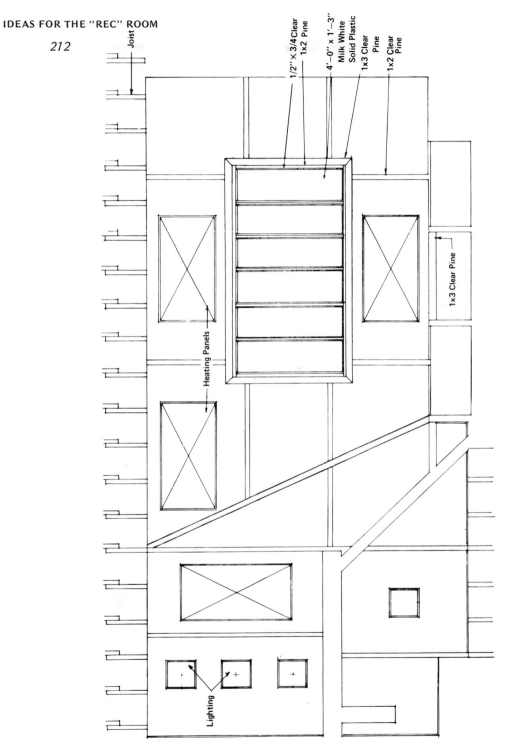

Figure 11-42: Layout for a typical ceiling-lighting grid.

For the turned staircase, the two bottom treads were removed and the new design framed with 2 x 8s ripped to size. The frame was faced with 3/4″ kickplates. Evenly space the treads 1/8″ apart by using scraps between each tread while nailing it down.

Figure 11-43: The partition at the foot of the stairs hides a pipe while its pass-through allows long boards and panels to make the turn down into the work shop.

214

The pass-through partition shown at the foot of the stairs (pages 209 & 213) was designed specifically to hide a black, cast iron sewer pipe. It also created a foyer and enclosed the food service area, while allowing long boards and 4 x 8 panels to be brought downstairs and into the shop.

To build the pass-through partition, cut the two end uprights to length, and fasten them to a joist with carriage bolts and glue. Then make two similar but opposite hand frames. Swing the frames up into position, and tie them together with cross members. Fasten the frame to the wall, floor, ceiling, and uprights. Install the paneling and trim.

See additional specific notes below for framing the bedroom closets, bookcases, sewing center, and sliding barn doors.

Electrical Installations

After the ceiling blocking and framing are in place, staple aluminum foil into all fluorescent strip cavities. You should now do the rough wiring.

Two similarly constructed styles of 4 x 8 lighting grids are diagrammed below. The 4-foot dimension in the grid near the sewing center runs parallel to the joists. Six 4' light fixtures are fastened between each of the six joists in this unit. The 4'0" dimension in the grid in the workshop runs 90 degrees to the joists. Two 4' light fixtures are fastened end to end between each of the three joists. Also, a 1 x 2 brace divides the grid in the shop in half.

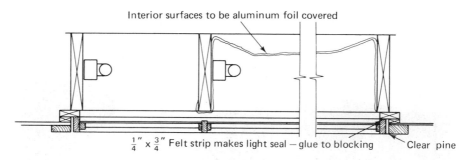

Interior surfaces to be aluminum foil covered

$\frac{1}{4}$" x $\frac{3}{4}$" Felt strip makes light seal — glue to blocking   Clear pine

Figure 11-44: Construction details for lighting grids (*top*) and for recessed heating units (*bottom*).

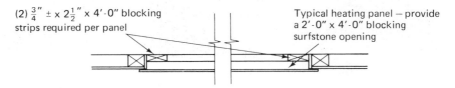

(2) $\frac{3}{4}$" ± x $2\frac{1}{2}$" x 4'-0" blocking strips required per panel

Typical heating panel — provide a 2'-0" x 4'-0" blocking surfstone opening

Cut the 1 x 2 grid frame pieces to size. Assemble the frame on the floor with 6d finishing nails and glue. Cut the 1/2" x 3/4" pieces of parting strip to length. Fasten these to the 1 x 2 frame with nails and glue while using scrap white plastic on the floor to hold the parting strip about 1/16" above the bottom edge of the 1 x 2 frame. Paint the grid black or stain it. Use a utility knife to cut the white plastic inserts to fit the grid, and install them. Fasten the black foam (or felt) light seal in place, and install the light grid with 1/4" lag bolts.

Paneling and Trim

Masonite Coach House White paneling is used here. Saw the paneling to fit the height of your walls. Cut the baseboard to a uniform width—about 5-1/2" deep—so it matches the pine baseboard trim of the sliding doors when they are hung and so the middle rail of this paneling blends well with other architectural features. Also, plan for the location of the vertical stile in this paneling, or saw it off so the stile does not butt against a vertical trim board.

Use 2 x 3s laid on a sawhorse to support the 4 x 8 paneling while sawing it. If you use a portable circular saw, set it to cut about 3/8" deep. Use the factory edge of a 10" to 20" wide piece of 3/4" thick particleboard to make a straight rip fence. Hold the rip fence in position with clamps at both ends.

Follow the installation directions printed on the protective covering of each panel. Three joint treatments may be used where the paneling joins the trim: (1) Butt the paneling against the molding; (2) Butt the panels together and cover the joint with a trim board; (3) Cut a 1/4" x 1/4" rabbet in the trim board to cover the edge of the paneling.

The inside corner joints of the tileboard in the closet, bookcases, and sewing center are 90-degree butts. Therefore, measure and cut these carefully. You can "fudge" on these joints a little by running a fine bead of white silicone tub calk, smoothed with your index finger, along the joint. Also, use nails sparingly—rely on the panel adhesive. Wherever possible, place nails so they will be hidden behind the shelf standards.

Cut the ceiling panels to fit your plan. Do not butt the panels tightly; leave an expansion gap. Cut the access holes wherever electrical junction boxes occur. (Cover these holes with 6" diameter junction box covers painted to blend with the ceiling material.) Also cut access holes for water valves and clean-outs.

Fasten paneling to the ceiling blocking with general purpose adhesive applied generously and with 1″ colored nails spaced every 4 inches.

Trim the ceiling, then the walls. As you cut each piece of ceiling or wall trim to size, sand out the planer ripple marks and erase pencil marks. Remove dents by applying a wet rag on the depression and pressing it with a soldering iron. The steam created will bring out the dent. Stain the board according to the instructions below. Then fasten the board in place with 6d or 8d finishing nails and set them. The false beams, which hide drain pipes, are simple boxes nailed and glued together, and fastened to ceiling blocking specifically constructed for them. Cut clear pine to fit between the window trim boards and the furring, and install. Miter the 1 x 3 trim around the light grid.

Plastic resin glue is recommended whenever you glue pine that will be stained. Use a hot, wet rag to wipe away the excess glue that squeezes out. Dilute your stain with one-third mineral spirits, and slop it on the boards generously with an old brush. Experiment with the amount of mineral spirits to add to get the desired shade. Wipe off the excess stain promptly with a rag to achieve the even shade desired. When dry, varnish the wood.

Fill nail holes with pre-colored wood putty after the first coat of varnish has dried. Use your index finger to apply it. After 24 hours, remove the excess putty and smooth it by wiping clean with a damp rag. After 24 hours, apply a second coat of varnish.

Flooring

The flooring material used in this basement is Spring pattern Shinyl Vinyl. When the concrete basement floor is in good shape, as this one was, the floor covering can be laid right over it. Instructions for sheet vinyl installation are given in Chapter 7.

Platform Beds

Fur out the walls with 2 x 2s as described earlier. Install an electrical convenience outlet 15-1/2″ above the floor (on the wall between the beds, above the shelf).

Build framing for the platform beds, legs, and shelf as a unit, following Figure 11-45. Assemble the framing with 10d nails, and reinforce the corners with steel braces. Cut the trim next. Notch the 1 x 3 front trim for the shelf so that it fits over the 2 x 3s and 2 x 2s that extend from the bed. Use 6d finishing nails and plastic resin glue to fasten all 1 x 3 horizontal trim boards.

Put the frame into position, and fasten it to the wall with 1/4″ lag bolts. Glue and nail scrap pieces of 1/4″ thick paneling on

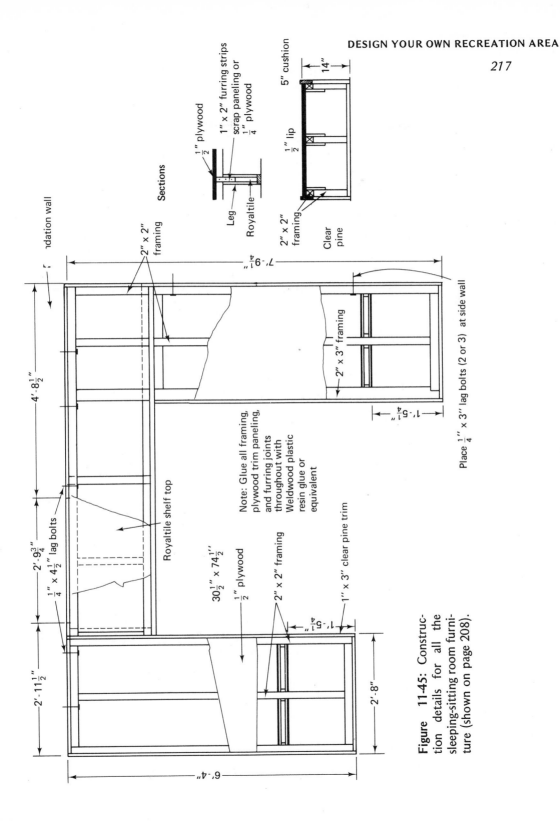

Sections

$\frac{1}{2}''$ plywood

$1'' \times 2''$ furring strips

scrap paneling or $\frac{1}{4}''$ plywood

Leg

Royaltile

5" cushion

14"

$\frac{1}{2}''$ lip

$2'' \times 2''$ framing

Clear pine

ndation wall

$2'' \times 2''$ framing

7'-9$\frac{1}{4}''$

$2'' \times 3''$ framing

1'-5$\frac{1}{4}''$

Place $\frac{1}{4}'' \times 3''$ lag bolts (2 or 3) at side wall

4'-8$\frac{1}{2}''$

Royaltile shelf top

2'-9$\frac{3}{4}''$ lag bolts

$\frac{1}{4}'' \times 4\frac{1}{2}''$ lag bolts

Note: Glue all framing, plywood trim paneling, and furring joints throughout with Weldwood plastic resin glue or equivalent

30$\frac{1}{2}'' \times 74\frac{1}{2}''$

$\frac{1}{2}''$ plywood

$2'' \times 2''$ framing

$1'' \times 3''$ clear pine trim

1'-5$\frac{1}{4}''$

2'-11$\frac{1}{2}''$

2'-8"

6'-4"

Figure 11-45: Construction details for all the sleeping-sitting room furniture (shown on page 208).

218   either side of the leg frames to shim them out. Then cover both sides with paneling so it is flush with the trim. Nail vertical trim on the legs.

Glue and nail 1/2" thick plywood sheets to the bed frames. Cover the shelf frame with 3/4" particleboard. Cover the particleboard with paneling, gluing it down with panel adhesive. Sew zippered mattress covers for the 5" thick foam mattresses to complete the beds.

Slide-Away Tables

Design these tables to fit under the counters with about an inch of clearance on all sides. Start construction by cutting the 1-1/4" × 2" notches for the legs in the particleboard. The clear white pine stock should be a full 2" × 2" for the trestle. Plane or smooth the pieces as necessary. Then cut the legs and "H" frame stretchers to length.

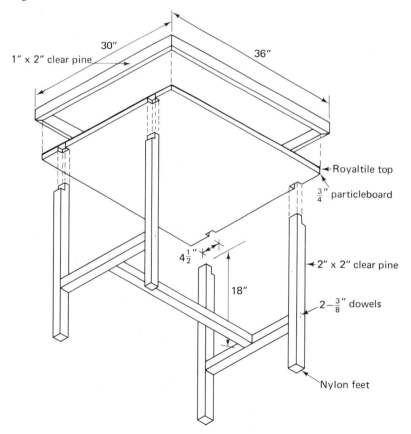

Figure 11-46: Complete diagram for making the slide-away study tables.

Assemble the H frame by using the notched particleboard top as a pattern. Clamp the two end pieces of the frame to the particleboard surface so that they line up with the edges of their respective notches. Bore the double dowel holes through each end and 1″ deep into the cross bar. Cut four dowel pins 3-1/4″ long. Coat the holes with plastic resin glue, and drive the dowels home. Wipe off the excess glue with a wet rag. (The dowels should protrude 1/4″ and will be cut flush later.) Keep the H frame stretcher clamped in position for 24 hours until the glue sets.

Cut the legs and the 3/4″ x 1-1/2″ tenons to length. Bore two 3/8″ holes through the legs and 1″ into the ends of the H frame. Cut the 3/8″ dowel pins to 3-1/4″ lengths and assemble the trestle dry.

Cut the tileboard next. Apply panel adhesive to the particleboard, place the tileboard on it, and weight it down. When dry, turn the table upside down, and fasten the legs in their notches with 6d finishing nails and plastic resin glue. Put the same glue in the holes in the legs and drive in the dowels. While the table is upside down, use bar clamps if necessary to keep the two diagonals between the legs equal to insure square. Also, use a framing square to be sure that all legs are 90 degrees to the top.

When the glue has set, turn the table over. Cut the mitered 1 x 2 edge border, and fasten it with 6d nails and plastic resin glue. Saw off the dowels to within 1/16″ of the leg surfaces. Then pare the dowel flush to the surface with a sharp, 1/2″ chisel. As you pare, tap the chisel toward the center of the dowel. Drive nylon furniture glides into each leg. Sand and finish.

Sliding Barn Doors

Two examples of framing for the sliding door track—parallel to the I-beams and parallel to the joists—are illustrated in Figure 11-47. There is one lap joint in the frames to accommodate the offset of the joists on either side of the I-beam. Be sure that the 1 x 12 trim board will cover your framing design.

Cut the 2 x 3s and 2 x 2s to size and assemble them on your pattern with nails and plastic resin glue. Also, saw out gussets from scrap paneling, and nail and glue them to reinforce the notched butt joint.

After the glue has set 24 hours, fasten the frames to the joists, or ceiling blocking, with 1/4″ x 3-1/2″ carriage bolts and white glue. Mark the locations of the first and last frames, and fasten them in place. Then tie four taut strings between the two frames (top and bottom on each side) to guide the location of the intermediate frames.

When the framing is up and the glue has set, use white glue and 8d finishing nails to fasten the trim boards to the frames. Start with the bottom boards (if there is not a partition); the width of the frame may require two boards. Then install the three boards that form the track channel.

Paneling the Barn Doors: Panel both sides of doors that divide the two living areas, such as those enclosing the sleeping area. Panel only the faces of doors enclosing areas such as the workshop. Paint the panel backs of the latter doors with off-white enamel. The horizontal rails in the front of the barn doors fit between the stiles; they do not go across the width of the door. The back of the door is constructed in the opposite manner; the rails do go across the width of the door.

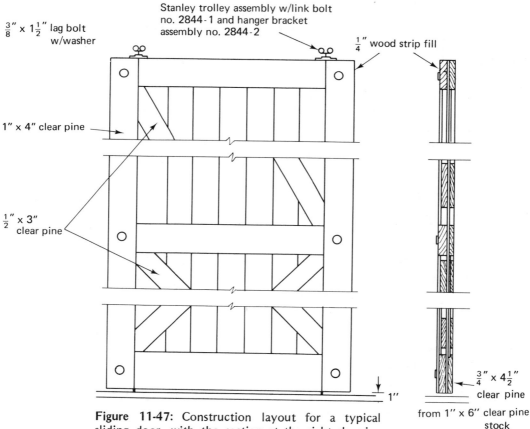

Figure 11-47: Construction layout for a typical sliding door, with the section at the right showing assembly details.

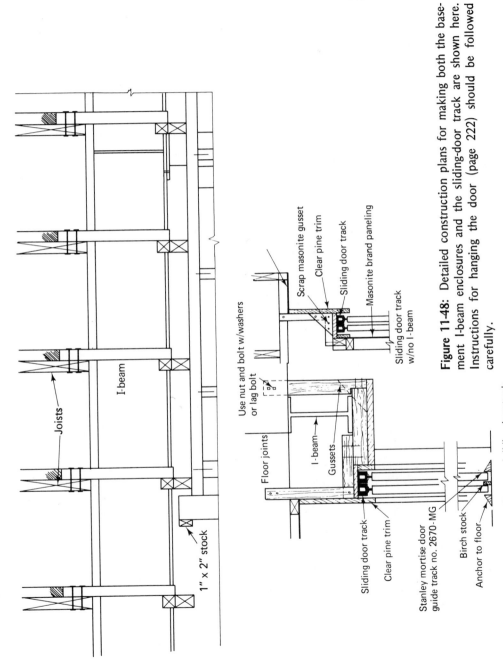

Joists

I-beam

1" x 2" stock

Scrap masonite gusset

Clear pine trim

Sliding door track

Masonite brand paneling

Sliding door track w/no I-beam

Use nut and bolt w/washers or lag bolt

Floor joints

I-beam

Gussets

Sliding door track

Clear pine trim

Stanley mortise door guide track no. 2670-MG

Birch stock

Anchor to floor

Typical I-beam enclosure and sliding door track

Figure 11-48: Detailed construction plans for making both the basement I-beam enclosures and the sliding-door track are shown here. Instructions for hanging the door (page 222) should be followed carefully.

Determine the size of the doors for your opening. Cut the clear pine boards to size per plan, and stain them before fabricating the doors. If Coach House paneling is used, make the middle rail 3-7/8" wide to cover the rail pattern in that paneling. If the door is double faced, cut a rabbet 1/4" deep and 1/2" wide for the paneling on the interior side to fit into. For these doors, the middle rail on the back is 1/2"-thick stock. If there are three sliding doors to cover an area, omit the single cross piece in the front side of the upper section of the middle door. The cross buck members are not necessary on door backs.

Cut the paneling to size—1" narrower than the door, or to fit the rabbeted stiles. Assemble the doors with panel adhesive and 3/8" lag screws and washers. Use 6d finishing nails as required to clamp the 1 x 4 framing together.

Fill the 1/4" gap between 1 x 4s by gluing in lattice and planing it flush later, when dry. Stack the doors on a flat surface for 24 hours until the glue sets.

Hanging the Doors: Install the upper and lower hardware on the doors. Turn the hardware slightly so that the screws are driven into wood and do not wedge the frames apart.

Screw the upper track to the center of the track channel. Drop a plumb bob from the center of the inside track at each end to establish the center line of that track on the floor. Snap a chalk line on the floor. Hang the doors that go on the inside track. Slide the U-shaped mortise door guide track in place, and center the holes over the chalk line. Mark the location of the holes. Drill and bolt U-tracks down with lead anchors spaced at least every 24 inches. Cut the 1-1/2 x 3/4" center strip of birch threshold to length; stain it and cement it down with panel adhesive. Hang the outer door, and slide the U-channel into place. Hold the outer channel tight against the center birch strip, and mark the bolt holes. Install lead anchors and bolt them down. Chamfer both outer pieces of 3/4 x 1-1/2" birch threshold to form triangular cross-sections as diagrammed on page 221. Stain and fasten the sections in place with epoxy glue.

Adjust leveling screws so the doors match in height and are plumb. Fill the nail holes, and varnish the doors.

New Living Space from Porches

12 & Garages

Generally speaking, it is easier and cheaper to finish an attic or a basement than it is to create new space by enclosing a porch. Basements and attics are already fully enclosed and weatherproof, while you will have to erect outside walls on a porch. A garage, while not requiring the building of outside walls (at least on three sides), presents some other structural problems, particularly in the area of the existing doors.

On the other hand, a finished-off porch or garage will yield a much greater return at resale time than most attics and basements. Ground-floor living space is more valuable than second-floor area, and even more so in comparison to a finished third floor. As previously discussed, an improved basement area is worth little or nothing on resale.

ENCLOSING A GARAGE

Finishing off a garage, of course, brings up the immediate question of what to do with your car. But think for a moment—how many nights during the year does the car actually use its berth in the garage? Many, if not most, attached garages are actually oversized storage rooms, cluttered with lawnmowers, old newspapers, bicycles, gardening materials and equipment, old furniture, and general junk (which is one of the reasons people periodically have "garage sales"—just to clear out the accumulation).

Figure 12-1: This underutilized garage is on its way to becoming a much used family room.

Even if you do use your garage for its intended purpose of protecting the car from the elements, you might decide that it could better serve as additional living space. In that case, depending on the siting of your house on its lot, you might build or have built a new garage at the end or in front of the converted garage. Or you might build a detached garage elsewhere on the lot. For storage of lawn and garden gear and such items as bicycles, you can build a small shed, either attached to the back of the house or in a remote corner of the yard. As for old newspapers, broken furniture, and just plain junk—well, where would you put them if you lived in an apartment or a house without a garage, or without an attic or basement, for that matter? Out with the trash, of course, which is where they belong. So putting the garage to work for the family really makes good sense.

Before finishing off a garage (or enclosing a porch), be sure to check local building codes, and obtain the necessary permits. Whenever you alter the exterior of your home, it is wise to pay strict attention to local statutes and strictures. Otherwise, you may end up having to undo what you have done.

Garage Door Openings

Removing a garage door is no problem; nor is framing in the opening to form a new wall. A 2 x 4 stud frame to fit the opening can be assembled in the driveway or on the garage floor, and then tilted up in place, as described in Chapter 4. The top plate is secured to the old garage door header, and studs at each end are nailed to the old door framing. The bottom plate is fastened to the concrete floor by the same methods used for fastening plates to basement floors (Chapter 4).

Figure 12-2: Handsomely re-done with efficient built-ins and easy-to-care-for tile flooring, this garage is now welcome new living space.

Plywood or other sheathing is nailed to the outside of the studs—and then the problem arises: how to match the exterior siding to the rest of the house. Even if you use the identical siding, it is more likely to look like a patch rather than a match.

One solution is to replace the siding on each side of the garage door with new siding to match that of the rest of the house, and then paint the whole side of the house, both old siding and new. Having gone that far, you might as well paint the whole house so that all sides match.

If you are not ready to paint the entire house, or if the house is constructed of a material that you can't match (weathered brick, for example), the solution might be to use a material that is entirely different to provide a complement or contrast to the main part of the house. Be careful, though—some material textures and colors harmonize well; others clash to create an esthetic disaster. Before selecting the new siding, muster your drawing skills and make several sketches to see how the proposed new material will work with, or against, the existing siding.

Still another possibility for solving the garage door problem is to install a large picture window taking up the full width of the opening. The area below the window can then be finished in a

226 contrasting siding. Or a stone or brick planter can be built below the window. Even shrubs and other plantings could be used to hide the mismatched siding after the old driveway has been removed.

Figure 12-3: This unattractive, long and narrow one-car garage did not overwhelm its determined owner. Its potential living space was recognized and utilized.

Floors and Subfloors

In most areas of the country, a concrete garage floor covered by tile, vinyl, or carpeting would be unsuitable for comfortable year-round use. A new subfloor structure is required to keep out the cold.

If an attached garage is a step or two down from the main part of the house, as is often the case, you can build up the garage floor level, or nearly level, with the main floor. First, attach a 2 x 6, 2 x 8 or 2 x 10 ledger (depending on how much the floor will be raised as well as the span across the floor) to the house wall 5/8" plus the thickness of the finished flooring below the desired floor level. Make sure that it is perfectly level. Attach a similar ledger to the opposite wall of the garage, at the same level.

Figure 12-4: With furring strips attached to the concrete block, the determined owner paneled the garage walls with pre-finished hardboard (after fastening insulation between the furring strips). A small bathroom was then installed at one end and an elderly parent had a cozy private apartment without "young" noise (*courtesy of Masonite Corporation*).

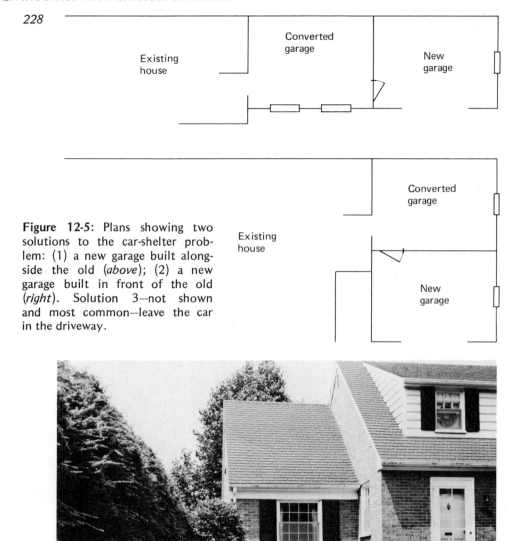

Figure 12-5: Plans showing two solutions to the car-shelter problem: (1) a new garage built alongside the old (*above*); (2) a new garage built in front of the old (*right*). Solution 3—not shown and most common—leave the car in the driveway.

Figure 12-6: Solution for the garage-door problem found by one fortunate homeowner; old brick that closely matches the rest of the house. The only "clue" to the former garage is the dead-end driveway.

Figure 12-7: A functional but not attractive solution to the garage-door problem: use of contrasting stonework that conspicuously fills in the wall of the former garage. Plantings would help—and removal of the stained concrete.

Lay a vapor barrier of polyethylene sheeting over the entire floor. Starting at one end of the garage, toenail a joist (the same dimensions as the ledgers) between the two ledgers, nailing it to the end wall studs as well. Measure 16″ from the end wall to the center of the second joist, then 16″ from center to center of the remaining joists. Finally, nail a joist in place at the opposite end wall.

Raising the floor allows you to run heating ducts or pipes under the floor to registers or convectors on the outer wall of the new room, where they will do the most good. Rough these in before applying subflooring (see Chapter 9). Place insulation between the joists, resting it on the polyethylene sheet. Air space above the batts or blankets will serve as additional insulation for the floor.

Starting at the same end wall where you began to install the joists, nail 4 x 8′ panels of 5/8″ plywood subflooring to the joists. Install underlayment and finished flooring as described in Chapter 7.

In many homes, particularly those built on concrete slabs, the garage floor is at or near the level of the main floor. While the main house floor is warmed by pipes or ducts that were implanted before the concrete was poured, the garage floor enjoys no such advantage. When converting the garage to living space, you could raise the floor as above, making it a step above the main floor. But this is an awkward solution in most cases. Another way to minimize the chill of the cold concrete: install foamed plastic slabs and plywood underlayment. It provides built-in thermal insulation and only raises the floor level about two inches.

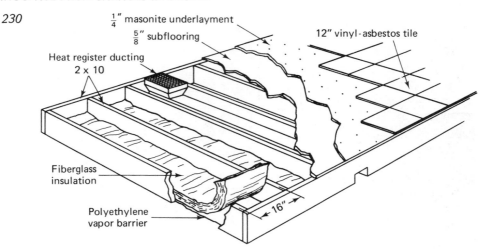

Figure 12-8: Raising the old garage floor will help keep the new space comfortable during cold weather.

Figure 12-9: Materials to begin a garage-to-living-space conversion include a large single-pane window (*against the rear wall*) and a three-pane unit (*at the right*). The latter will almost fill the garage door opening. The plywood and foam slabs are for the new floor (*courtesy of American Plywood Association*).

Check with your building supply dealer to make sure you use an adhesive that does not attack the plastic foam. Trowel the thick asphalt mastic, which doubles as a vapor barrier, onto the concrete, and then lay the foam slabs in place. Do this job a row at a time so you can avoid walking on the uncovered slabs and crushing them.

Figure 12-10: Once the plastic slabs are laid on the mastic-coated concrete (*above left*) trowel more mastic over them and put the underlayment panels in place (*above right*). Remember to kneel on a large piece of scrap lumber so that your weight spreads as you work; then you won't crush the foam. Finally, apply the finish flooring and enjoy your new space (*below*).

With three walls already in place and the former garage door opening framed in as above, little, if any, additional framing is required in your garage room. You may have to put in some new joists to fill in between the existing ones so that they are spaced 16" o.c. Use lumber of the same size as the existing joists, setting the new joists atop wall plates and nailing them to the plates and rafters.

Partitions, if there are to be any in your new room, are built as described in Chapter 4.

Since the walls and ceiling of a garage are normally unfinished, it is a simple matter to run cables through the ceiling to the outer walls for new electrical outlets and switches, following instructions given in Chapter 8. If the garage floor is not being raised as described above, heating pipes and ducts can also be run overhead. However, if the furnace is located in the basement, it is usually best to simply install heat outlets on the inside wall of the new room, next to the main part of the house. See Chapter 9 for details.

Insulation in the ceiling and outer walls of the converted garage room is a must (see Chapter 5). Install it before the finishing.

A GARAGE CONVERSION

Drawings and plans on the next three pages show how a garage was converted to a full-time family fun room and solarium. It was designed by architect James Otis for the Western Wood Products

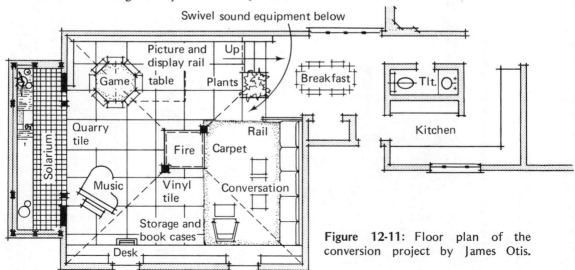

Figure 12-11: Floor plan of the conversion project by James Otis.

Figure 12-12: View from the breakfast area.

Association, and it is presented here to illustrate just what you can do with a garage—with ideas that you can adopt or adapt to fit your own needs and situation.

The former utility area between the kitchen and the garage became a breakfast nook and entry to the new room. The garage itself was zoned into various activity areas, with a central fireplace as the room's focal point, drawing them all together as a unit. The fireplace combines common brick with stone trim and random-width vertical wood strips for a striking effect.

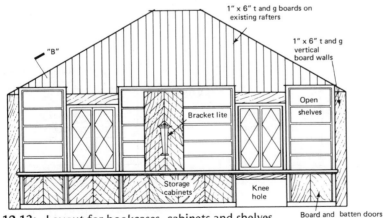

Figure 12-13: Layout for bookcases, cabinets and shelves.

The storage-and-bookcase wall introduces a herringbone pattern to counterpoint the verticals that dominate the room. Adjustable shelves accommodate items of various sizes with complete flexibility.

234   The large room is made to appear even more spacious by carrying the ceiling up to the full height of the hip roof; 1×6 tongue-and-groove ceiling boards are fastened to furring strips nailed across the existing rafters, giving a soaring effect.

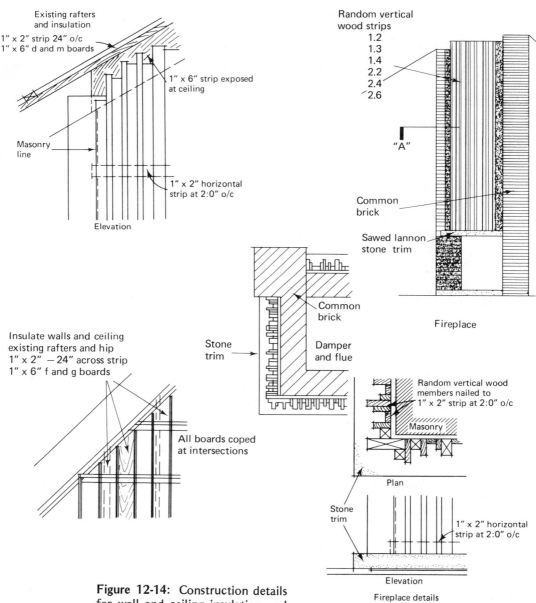

Figure 12-14: Construction details for wall and ceiling insulation and paneling and the central fireplace.

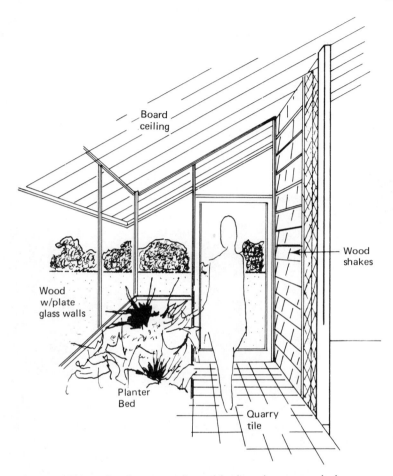

Figure 12-15: On the garage-door side there is now a solarium.

Perhaps the most ingenious innovation is the solarium, which supplies abundant natural light and greenery, even during the dreary winter months, along with potting area and storage space for gardening tools. Better yet, the solarium eliminates the need to wall up the hole left by the old garage door—a most effective solution to that problem.

ENCLOSING A PORCH

A porch may be a pleasant place to sit and rock on a summer night, but it is next to useless for a large part of the year in most climates. Enclosing it is a quick way to add living space to your home.

Many porches are built over a crawl space. Any dampness problems should be eliminated before enclosing the porch. Details are given in Chapter 3. Insulated heating ducts or pipes can be run between joists in the crawl space (see Chapter 9), and the floor should be insulated.

If the crawl space itself is not enclosed, with the porch simply resting on piers, this situation should be remedied. First, check all wood structural members for signs of rot or damage, and repair or replace them as necessary. Pour a concrete footing all

Figure 12-16: A porch that was pleasant and useful only in warm weather is now an all-weather, all-year round living space—with wood-framed sliding glass doors (*courtesy of Pella Corporation*).

Figure 12-17: You don't have to live in outer suburbia to re-cycle a porch. This transformation of the rear porches of an old inner-city walkup was made possible with redwood and glass—used generously.

around the perimeter of the porch, and build a wall of brick or concrete block to close off the crawl space. This will also help to control dampness under the porch room.

Some porches are built on concrete slabs. If you intend to enclose such a porch, the floor should first be treated just as you would treat a garage floor—either built up or insulated with foam slabs, as described earlier in this chapter.

Since a porch already has a roof, all you need do is erect 2 x 4 stud framing for one, two, or three walls, following the techniques outlined in Chapter 4. Matching existing exterior siding may pose a problem similar to that discussed earlier under "Garage Door Openings." The solutions are also similar. If you can't exactly match existing siding, it is probably better to select a completely different

238 material, providing an accent to the house's exterior appearance. Again, exercise judicious caution in selecting materials, and make sure that they work together, not at cross-purposes.

Other techniques for enclosing a porch—insulating, wiring, heating, finishing—are the same as those discussed elsewhere in this book for finishing off any area of the house.

ONE MAN'S FAMILY—AND ENCLOSING A PORCH

Kenny Mann, a widower with one child, gained an instant larger family when he married Katie, a widow with three children. Since Kenny lived in a delightful but small former summer home on Long Island, New York, he and Katie needed more room—fast.

Kenny's cottage, although small, had already undergone several expansions. One of these included the addition of a long back porch overlooking a spacious yard to the side and rear filled with

Figure 12-18: The old back porch—pleasant enough but needed for more important purposes.

lovely flowering dogwood trees. Kenny decided to convert the old porch to a bedroom–sitting room for himself and his bride, which would allow the rearranging of other rooms inside the house to accommodate the children.

Since the porch was built on a sturdy concrete block foundation, that posed no problem. Kenny dampproofed the crawl space, insulated the floor, and ran two insulated heat ducts to the porch from the forced-air furnace in the basement.

Figure 12-19: This photograph shows construction under way. The differences in shingle coloring (*left*) identify a previous, somewhat careless addition that included the porch now being enclosed.

To retain the superb view, as well as to admit maximum light, Kenny installed large casement windows on both sides and the rear of the former porch. To the rear, he added sliding glass doors, which will (in the near future, he says) open onto a new wood deck. Both windows and doors are thermal-insulating types—Long Island winters can be bitterly cold. But the summers can also be (and usually are) balmy, so windows and doors are fitted with screens so that they can be opened to admit the refreshing breezes that blow off Long Island Sound.

240   Normal 2×4 stud framing was erected between the window and door units. Kenny didn't bother to try matching the shingle siding on the existing house (the job had already been botched once on an addition made by a former owner). Instead, he applied vertical pine paneling, nailed to furring strips on the studs, providing a handsome asymmetrical look to the back and sides of the house.

Figure 12-20: The photograph shows the enclosed porch with its new vertical pine siding. The old stairs remained temporarily in place until a wood deck was built. *If* it had been left this way, the high foundation would have needed close planting with some fairly large evergreens.

Figure 12-21: Large glass areas inside the new bedroom admit plenty of light and give a lovely view of the wooded area outside.

All in all, a very pleasant "honeymoon cottage" for Kenny, Katie, and their growing family—and an excellent example of how to make better use of existing space in the home.

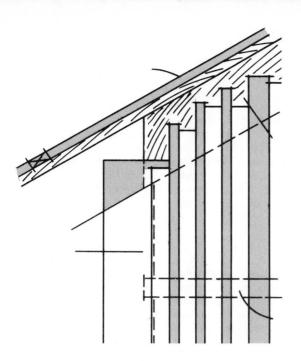

Glossary

Airway: a space between the roof insulation and the roof boards for movement of air.

Alternating current (AC): current that changes its direction of flow through a conductor, going first one way, then the other; the usual rate used is 60 alternations (60 times each way) per second.

Ampere (amp): the unit for measuring electrical current's rate of flow.

Apron: the flat member of the inside trim of a window placed against the wall immediately beneath the stool (see below).

Asphalt: most native asphalt is a residue from evaporated petroleum; insoluble in water but soluble in gasoline, it melts when heated. Asphalt is widely used in building for such items as waterproof roof coverings of many types, exterior wall coverings, and flooring tile.

Attic ventilator: in houses, the screened opening provided to ventilate an attic space; located in the soffit area as *inlet ventilators*, and in the gable end or along the ridge as *outlet ventilators*; they can also consist of power-driven fans used as an exhaust system. *See also* **Louver**.

Backfill: the replacement of excavated earth into a trench or pier excavation around and against a basement foundation.

Baluster: usually the small vertical member in a railing used between the top rail and the stair treads or the bottom rail.

Base or baseboard: a board placed around a room against the wall and next to the floor to finish properly between the floor and the plaster or drywall.

Base molding: molding used to trim the upper edge of the interior baseboard.

Base shoe: molding used next to the floor on interior baseboards; sometimes called a *carpet strip*.

Batten: a narrow strip of wood used to cover joints or as a decorative vertical member over plywood or wide boards.

Beam: a structural member transversely supporting a load.

Bearing wall: a wall that supports any vertical load in addition to its own weight.

Bed molding: a molding in an angle, as between the overhanging cornice, or eaves, of a building and the sidewalls.

Blind-nailing: nailing in such a way that the nailheads are not visible on the face of the work; usually at the tongue of matched boards. *See* **Lumber, matched.**

Blind stop: a rectangular molding, usually 3/4" x 1-3/8" or more in width, used in the assembly of a window frame; it serves as a stop for storm and screen or combination windows and to resist air infiltration.

Bolt, anchor: bolts used to secure a wooden sill plate to a concrete or masonry floor or a wall or pier.

Brace: an inclined piece of framing lumber applied to a wall or floor to stiffen the structure; often used on walls as temporary bracing until framing has been completed.

Built-up roof: a roofing composed of three to five layers of asphalt felt laminated with coal tar, pitch, or asphalt; the top is finished with crushed slag or gravel; generally used on flat or low-pitched roofs.

Butt joint: the junction where the ends of two timbers or other members meet in a square-cut joint.

Cabinet: a shop- or job-built unit for kitchens or other rooms; often includes combinations of drawers, doors, and the like.

Casement frame and sash: a frame of wood or metal enclosing all or part of the sash and which may be opened by means of hinges affixed to the vertical edges.

Casing: molding of various widths and thicknesses used to trim door and window openings at the jambs.

Collar beam: a nominal 1" or 2" thick member connecting opposite roof rafters; it stiffens the roof.

Combination door or window: combination door or window used over a regular opening to provide winter insulation and summer protection; often has self-storing or removable glass and screen inserts which eliminate the need for a different unit each season.

Condensation: beads or drops of water, and frequently frost in extremely cold weather, that accumulate on the inside of the exterior covering of a building when warm, moisture-laden air from the interior reaches a point where the temperature no longer permits the air to contain its moisture.

Conduit, electrical: a pipe, usually metal, in which wire is installed.

Construction, drywall: a type of construction in which the interior wall finish is applied in a dry condition, generally in the form of gypsum sheet materials or wood paneling, as contrasted to plaster.

Construction, frame: a type of construction in which the structural parts are of wood or depend upon a wood frame for support; if masonry veneer is applied to the exterior walls, the classification of this type of construction is usually unchanged in building codes.

Convector: a baseboard heater that transfers warmth from hot water to the air.

Coped joint: woodwork fitted to an irregular surface. In moldings, coping means cutting the end of one piece to fit the molded face of the other at an interior angle to replace a miter joint.

Corner bead: a strip of formed sheet metal, sometimes combined with a strip of metal lath, placed on corners before plastering to reinforce them; also, a strip of wood finish, either three-quarters round or angular, placed over a plastered corner for protection.

Corner board: used as trim for the external corners of a house or other frame structure against which the ends of the siding are finished.

Corner brace: diagonal brace at the corners of a frame structure to stiffen and strengthen the wall.

Cornice: overhang of a pitched roof at the eave line; usually consisting of a facia board (see below), a soffit (see below) for a closed cornice, and appropriate moldings.

Counterflashing: a flashing usually used on chimneys at the roofline to cover shingle flashing and to prevent entry of moisture.

Cove molding: a molding with a concave face used to trim or to finish interior corners.

Crawl space: a shallow space below the living quarters of a basementless house, sometimes enclosed.

d. *See* **Penny.**

Dado: a rectangular groove cut across the width of a board or plank.

Deck paint: an enamel paint with a high degree of resistance to mechanical wear, designed for use on such surfaces as porch floors.

Density: the mass of substance in a unit volume; when expressed in the metric system (in grams per cubic centimeter), it is numerically equal to the specific gravity of the same substance.

Diffuser: a baseboard unit into which warm air is fed and spread throughout a room.

Dimension. *See* **Lumber, dimension.**

Direct current (DC): electric current without alternations, flows in one direction only.

Door jamb, interior: the surrounding case into and out of which a door closes and opens; it consists of two upright pieces, called *side jambs*, and a horizontal *head jamb*.

Dormer: a projection in a sloping roof, the framing of which forms a vertical wall suitable for windows or other openings; usually built to add attic headroom.

Downspout: a pipe, usually made of metal, for carrying rainwater from roof gutters.

Drip cap: a molding placed on the exterior top side of a door or window frame to cause water to drip beyond the outside of the frame.

Drywall. *See* **Construction, drywall.**

Duct: in a house, usually a round or rectangular metal pipe for distributing warm air from the heating plant, or cool air from an air conditioning device, to rooms or for returning cold air; ducts are also made of asbestos and composition materials.

Eaves: the lower border of a roof that overhangs the wall.

Face-nailing: to nail perpendicular to the initial surface or to the junction of the pieces joined.

Facia or fascia: a flat board, band, or face, used sometimes by itself but usually in combination with moldings; often located at the outer face of the cornice.

Filament: the threadlike tungsten wire that incandesces or lights up when an electric current runs through it; the light source in an incandescent lamp.

Flashing: sheet metal or other material used in roof and wall construction to protect a building from seepage of water.

Flat paint: an interior paint with a high proportion of pigment; dries to a flat or lusterless finish.

Flue: the passageway in a chimney through which smoke, gas, or fumes ascend; each passageway is called a flue, which together with any others and the surrounding masonry make up the chimney.

Flue lining: fire clay or terra cotta pipe, round or square, usually made in all of the ordinary flue sizes and in 2' lengths; used for the inner lining of chimneys with a brick or masonry work around the outside; the flue lining runs from about a foot below the flue connection to the top of the chimney.

Footcandle: the unit of illumination: one footcandle is one lumen per square foot.

Footing: a masonry section, usually concrete, rectangular; wider than the bottom of the foundation wall or pier it supports.

Foundation: the supporting portion of a structure below the first-floor construction, or below grade, including the footings.

Framing, balloon: a system of framing a building in which all vertical structural elements of the bearing walls and partitions consist of single pieces extending from the top of the foundation sill plate to the roofplate and to which all floor joists are fastened.

Framing, platform: a system of framing a building in which floor joists of each story rest on the top plates of the story below or on the foundation sill for the first story, and the bearing walls and partitions rest on the subfloor of each story.

Frieze: in house construction, a horizontal member connecting the top of the siding (see below) and the soffit (see below) of the cornice or roof sheathing.

Frostline: the depth of frost penetration in soil; varies in different parts of the country. Footings should be placed below this depth to prevent movement.

Furring: strips of wood or metal applied to a wall or other surface to even it and usually to serve as a fastening base for finish material.

Gable: the triangular vertical end of a building formed by the eaves and ridge of a sloped roof; a type of dormer.

Girder: a large or principal beam of wood or steel used to support concentrated loads at isolated points along its length.

Gloss (paint or enamel): a paint or enamel that contains a relatively low proportion of pigment and dries to a sheen or luster.

Grain: the direction, size, arrangement, appearance, or quality of the fibers in wood.

Grain, edge (vertical): edge-grain lumber that has been sawed parallel to the pith of the log and approximately at right angles to the growth rings; that is, the rings form an angle of 45° or more with the surface of the piece.

Gusset: a flat wood, plywood, or similar type member used to provide a connection at the intersection of wood members and fastened by nails, screws, bolts, or adhesives; most commonly used at joints of wood trusses.

Gutter or eave trough: a shallow channel or conduit of metal or wood set below and along the eaves of a house to catch and carry off rainwater from the roof.

Header: (*a*) a beam placed perpendicular to joists and to which joists are nailed in framing for chimney, stairway, or other opening; (*b*) a wood lintel.

Heartwood: the wood extending from the pith to the sapwood, the cells of which no longer participate in the life processes of the tree.

Heat fin: a metal plate, usually aluminum, that clamps over hot water lines to provide heat to basements.

Hip: the external angle formed by the meeting of two sloping sides of a roof.

Hip roof: a roof that rises by inclined planes from all four sides of a building.

Insulation, thermal: any material high in resistance to heat transmission that, when placed in the walls, ceilings, or floors of a structure, will reduce the rate of heat flow.

Insulation board, rigid: a structural building board made of wood or cane fiber in 1/2″ and 25/32″ thicknesses; can be obtained in various size sheets, in various densities, and with several treatments.

Jamb: the side and head lining of a doorway, window, or other opening.

Joint: the space between the adjacent surfaces of two members or components held together by nails, glue, cement, mortar, or other means.

Joint cement: a powder that is usually mixed with water and used for joint treatment in gypsum wallboard finish; often called *spackle*.

Joist: one of a series of parallel beams, usually a nominal 2″ thick by 6″ wide; used to support floor and ceiling loads, and supported in turn by larger beams, girders, or bearing walls.

Kneewall: a low wall formed by attaching studs between the rafters and floor of an attic; usually shorter than normal walls.

Knot: in lumber, the section of the base of a branch or limb of a tree that appears on the edge or face of the piece.

Landing: a platform between flights of stairs or at the termination of a flight of stairs.

Lath: a building material of wood, metal, gypsum, or insulating board that is fastened to the frame of a building to act as a plaster base.

Ledger strip: a strip of lumber nailed along the bottom of the side of a girder on which joists rest.

Light: space in a window sash for a single pane of glass; also, a pane of glass.

Lintel: a horizontal structural member that supports the load over an opening such as a door or window.

Louver: an opening with a series of horizontal slats so arranged as to permit ventilation but to exclude rain, sunlight, or vision. *See also* **Attic ventilators.**

Lumber: lumber is the product of the sawmill and planing mill not further manufactured other than by sawing, resawing, and passing lengthwise through a standard planing machine, cross cutting to length, and matching.

Lumber, board: lumber less than 2″ thick and 2″ or more wide.

Lumber dimension: lumber from a nominal 2″ to, but not including 5″ thick, and 2″ or more wide; includes joists, rafters, studs, planks, and small timbers. The actual size of such lumber after shrinking from green dimension and after machining to size or pattern is called the *dressed size.*

Lumber, matched: lumber that is dressed and shaped on one edge in a grooved pattern and on the other in a tongued pattern.

Lumber, shiplap: lumber that is edge-dressed to make a close rabbeted or lapped joint.

Masonry: stone, brick, concrete, hollow tile, concrete block, gypsum block, or other similar building units or materials or a combination of the same, bonded together with mortar to form a wall, pier, buttress, or similar mass.

Meeting rail: rail sufficiently thicker than a window to fill the opening between the top and bottom sash made by the parting stop in the frame of double-hung windows; usually beveled.

Millwork: generally all building materials made of finished wood and manufactured in millwork plants and planing mills are included under the term *millwork* and including such items as inside and outside doors, window and door frames, blinds, porchwork, mantels, panelwork, stairways, moldings, and interior trim; normally does not include flooring, ceiling materials, or siding.

Miter joint: the joint of two pieces at an angle that bisects the joining angle; for example, the miter joint at the side and head casing at a door opening is made at a 45° angle.

Moisture content of wood: weight of the water contained in the wood, usually expressed as a percentage of the weight of the oven-dry wood.

Molding: a wood strip having a curved or projecting surface used for decorative purposes.

Mortise: a slot cut into a board, plank, or timber, usually edgewise, so as to receive a tenon of another board, plank, or timber to form a joint.

Natural finish: a transparent finish that does not seriously alter the original color or grain of the natural wood; usually provided by sealers, oils, varnishes, water-repellent preservatives, and other similar materials.

Non-load-bearing wall: a wall supporting no load other than its own weight.

Notch: a crosswise rabbet at the end of a board.

o.c. (on center): the measurement of spacing for studs, rafters, joists, and the like in a building; measured from the center of one member to the center of the next.

Ohm: measure of electrical resistance.

Paint: a combination of pigments with suitable thinners or oils to provide decorative and protective coatings.

Panel: in house construction, a thin flat piece of wood, plywood, or similar material; used for wall-covering, or framed by stiles and rails as in a door, or fitted in grooves of thicker material with molded edges.

Paper, sheathing or building: a building material, generally paper or felt, used in wall and roof construction as a protection against the passage of air and sometimes moisture.

Parting stop or strip: a small wood piece used in the side and head jambs of double-hung windows to separate the upper and lower sash.

Partition: a wall subdividing spaces within any story of a building.

Penny: as applied to nails, the term originally indicated the price per hundred; now serves as a measure of nail length; abbreviated as **d** from pence (*British*; denarii, *L.*).

Pier: a column of masonry, usually rectangular in horizontal cross-section and used to support other structural members.

Pigment: a powdered solid in suitable degree of subdivision for use in coloring paint or enamel.

Pitch: the incline slope of a roof, or the ratio of the total rise to the total width of a house; that is, an 8' rise and a 24' width give a 1/3 pitch roof (8:24). *Roof slope* is expressed in inches of rise per 12" of run.

Plate: *sill plate*: a horizontal member anchored to a masonry wall; *soleplate*: the bottom horizontal member of a frame wall; *top plate*: the top horizontal member of a frame wall supporting ceiling joists, rafters, or other members.

Plenum: sheet metal "bonnet" on top of the furnace that feeds heated air to branch ducts and pipes.

Plumb: of a surface, meaning exactly perpendicular or vertical; true in direction.

Plywood: a piece of wood made of three or more layers of veneer joined with glue and usually laid with the grain of adjoining plies at right angles. An odd number of plies is almost always used to provide balanced construction.

Porch: a roofed area extending beyond the main house; may be open or enclosed with concrete or wood-frame floor system.

Preservative: any substance that, for a reasonable length of time, will prevent the action of wood-destroying fungi, borers of various kinds, and similar destructive life when the wood has been properly coated or impregnated with it.

Primer: the first coat of paint in a paint job that consists of two or more coats; also the paint used for such a first coat.

Putty: a type of cement usually made of whiting and boiled linseed oil, beaten or kneaded to the consistency of dough, and used in sealing glass in sash, for filling small holes and crevices in wood, and for similar purposes.

Quarter round: a small molding with the shape of the cross-section of a quarter circle.

Rafter: one of a series of structural members of a roof designed to support roof loads; the rafters of a flat roof are sometimes called *roof joists*.

Rafter, hip: a rafter that forms the intersection of an external roof angle.

Rafter, jack: a rafter that spans the distance from the wallplate to a hip or from a valley to a ridge.

Rafter, valley: a rafter that forms the intersection of an internal roof angle; normally made of doubled 2" thick members.

Rail: cross member of a panel door or of a sash; also the upper and lower members of a balustrade or staircase extending from one vertical support, such as a post, to another.

Rake: the inclined edge of a gable roof; the trim member is called a *rake molding*.

Ridge: the horizontal line at the junction of the top edges of two sloping roof surfaces.

Ridge board: the board placed on edge at the ridge of the roof into which the upper ends of the rafters are fastened.

Rise: in stairs, the vertical height of a step or a flight of stairs.

Riser: each of the vertical boards closing the spaces between the treads (see below) of stairways; also a sheet-metal duct within a partition that carries heated air to a second floor.

Roll roofing: roofing material, composed of fiber and saturated with asphalt; supplied in rolls having 108 square feet in 36″ widths; generally furnished in weights of 45 to 90 pounds per roll.

Roof sheathing: the boards or sheet material fastened to the roof rafters and on which the shingles or other roof covering is laid.

Rout. *See* **Mortise.**

Run: in stairs, the net width of a step of the horizontal distance covered by a flight of stairs.

Sash: a single window frame containing one or more lights of glass.

Saturated felt: a felt that is impregnated with tar or asphalt.

Scab: a short piece of wood or plywood fastened to two abutting timbers to splice them together.

Sealer: a finishing material, either clear or pigmented, that is usually applied directly over uncoated wood for the purpose of sealing its surface.

Semi-gloss paint or enamel: a paint or enamel made with a slight insufficiency of nonvolatile vehicle so that its coating, when dry, has some luster but is not very glossy.

Shake: a thick handsplit shingle, resawed to form two shakes; usually edge grained.

Sheathing: the structural covering, usually wood boards or plywood, used over the studs or rafters of a structure. Structural building board is normally used only as wall sheathing.

Sheathing paper. *See* **Paper, sheathing or building.**

Shingle: roof covering of asphalt, asbestos, wood, tile, slate, or other material cut to stock lengths, widths, and thicknesses.

Shingle, siding: one of various kinds of shingles, such as wood shingles or shakes and nonwood shingles, that are used over sheathing for exterior sidewall covering of a structure.

Shiplap. *See* **Lumber, shiplap.**

Siding: the finish covering of the outside wall of a frame building, whether made of horizontal weatherboards, vertical boards with battens, shingles, or other material.

Siding, bevel (lap siding): wedge-shaped boards used as horizontal siding in a lapped pattern. This siding varies in butt thickness from 1/2″ to 3/4″ and in widths up to 12″; normally used over some type of sheathing.

Siding, drop: usually 3/4″ thick and 6″ or 8″ in width, with tongue-and-groove or shiplap edges; sometimes used as siding without sheathing, but not recommended for dwellings.

Siding, panel: large sheets of plywood or hardboard that serve as both sheathing and siding.

Sill: the lowest member of the frame of a structure, resting on the foundation and supporting the floor joists or the uprights of the wall; the member forming the lower side of an opening, as a door sill, window sill, etc.

Soffit: usually the underside covering of an overhanging cornice.

Soil cover (ground cover): a light covering of plastic film, roll roofing, or similar material used over the soil in crawl spaces of buildings to minimize moisture permeation of the area.

Soil stack: a general term for the vertical main of a system of soil, waste, or vent piping.

Sole or soleplate. *See* **Plate.**

Span: the distance between structural supports such as walls, columns, piers, beams, girders, and trusses.

Square: a unit of measure—for example, 100 square feet—usually applied to roofing material. Sidewall coverings are sometimes packed to cover 100 square feet and are sold on that basis.

Stain, shingle: a form of oil paint, very thin in consistency, intended for coloring rough-surfaced woods like shingles, without forming a coating or significant thickness or gloss.

Stair carriage: supporting member for stair treads; usually a 2″ plank notched to receive the treads; sometimes termed a *rough horse.*

Stool: a flat molding fitted over the window sill between the jambs and contacting the bottom rail of the lower sash.

Storm sash or storm window: an extra window usually placed on the outside of an existing window as additional protection against cold weather.

Story: that part of a building between any floor and the floor or roof above.

String, or stringer: a timber or other support for cross members in floors or ceilings; in stairs, the support on which the stair treads rest; also called *stringboard.*

Stud: one of a series of slender wood (usually 2×4) or metal vertical structural members placed as supporting elements in walls and partitions. (plural: *studs* or *studding*.)

Subfloor: boards or plywood laid on joists over which a finish floor is to be laid.

Tail beam: a relatively short beam or joist supported in a wall on one end and by a header at the other.

Termite shield: a shield, usually of noncorrodible metal, placed in or on a foundation wall or other mass of masonry or around pipes to prevent passage of termites.

Threshold: a strip of wood or metal with beveled edges used over the finished floor and the sill of exterior doors.

Toenailing: to drive a nail at a slant or angle to the initial surface in order to permit the nail to penetrate into a second member.

Tongue-and-groove. *See* **Lumber, matched.**

Tread: the horizontal board of a stairway on which the foot is placed.

Trim: the finish materials in a building, such as moldings, applied around openings (window trim and door trim) or at the floor and ceiling of rooms (baseboard, cornice, and picture molding).

Trimmer: a beam or joist to which a header is nailed for stairs, chimneys, or other openings in framing.

Truss: a frame or jointed structure designed to act as a beam of long span; each member is usually subjected to longitudinal stress only, either of tension or compression.

Turpentine: a volatile oil used as a thinner in paints and as a solvent in varnishes; chemically, a mixture of terpenes.

Undercoat: a coating applied prior to the finishing or top coats of paint; may be the first of two or the second of three coats. It may be used synonymously with *priming coat.*

Vapor barrier: material used to retard the movement of water vapor into walls and prevent condensation in them; applied separately over the warm side of exposed walls or as a part of batt or blanket insulation.

Varnish: a thickened preparation of drying oil or drying oil and resin suitable for spreading on surfaces to form continuous, transparent coatings, or for mixing with pigments to make enamels.

Vent: a pipe or duct that allows flow of air as in an inlet or outlet.

Vermiculite: a mineral closely related to mica, with the faculty of expanding on heating so as to form lightweight material with insulation qualities; used as bulk insulation, as aggregate in insulating and acoustical plaster, and in insulating concrete floors. (Also a soil conditioner.)

Volt: the measure of electromotive force.

Water-repellent preservative: a liquid designed to penetrate into wood and impart both water repellency and a moderate preservative protection; used for millwork, such as sash and frames, and is usually applied by dipping.

Watt: a measure of the work done by one ampere under the pressure of one volt.

Weatherstrip: narrow or jamb-width sections of thin metal or other material to prevent infiltration of air and moisture around windows and doors.

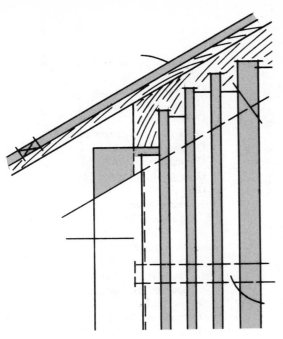

Index

*Page numbers in **boldface** indicate a definition of the indexed item.